While every precaution has been taken in the preparation of this book, the publisher assumes no responsibility for errors or omissions, or for damages resulting from the use of the information contained herein.

BE A MAN: LIVE A DISCIPLINED & HAPPY LIFE

**First edition. January 25, 2024.**



ISBN: 979-8224851393

Written by Martin Durst.

# Table of Contents

# Be a Man: Live a Disciplined & Happy Life

By
Martin G. Durst

# Dedication

This book is dedicated to my wife, Barbara, who allows me to be a godly man; my daughter, Emily, who always keeps my imagination alive; and to my son, Ethan, who loves to work with me and forgives me for being impatient.

# Introduction

What in the world is happening to American men? Over the past century we have traded our survival instincts, our grit, our warrior spirits, willingness to work, and the strength of our families for entertainment addiction, instant gratification, and entitlement pursuits. And in our pursuit for "social happiness," we have strayed too far.

This is a strong book. It's supposed to be; because most men are weak-willed, too soft-spoken, thin-skinned, uncommitted to their families, easily intimidated, civically stupid, mentally immature, and unwilling to grow up. Many live with the delusion that they can fix or hide from all these things by living in a fantasy world of media, sports, and games.

It's shameful and pathetic.

American men: Find your man card.

Many self-help books center on getting in shape and muscular development. Others books claim to help the reader identify with being a "modern male" and to be more sensitive. I was unable to find any books for men that explain how to deal with significant issues we all encounter day-to-day while not compromising our masculinity.

Men need to get a check-up-from-the-neck-up. We need to get off the couch, away from the television and game consoles, and be willing to put our families first before our own childish interests. Men have allowed America to become the land of governmental dependence, and the home of the lethargic. That's *not* what America was *ever* supposed to be.

THIS *is not* a book promoting male dominance over women. If you were hoping that was the case, you're mistaken. Men *are not* superior to woman. Without women, men are incomplete. Women are the balance to a man's aggressiveness and anger. They are the emotional anchor to remind us to have empathy when needed, and to show love to our children and not just stern discipline. Women are the other half that makes us whole.

Men should be leaders. That doesn't mean women can't lead. Women make good leaders too ... especially when men refuse to do so. But, if you are married, you should be willing to lead your wife, not act as a dictator.

This thinking may offend some, but it is the biblical recipe that creates harmony in the home. Harmony is what develops healthy and strong children. However, this *does not* imply that men are better than women. Men and women are one hundred percent equal partners in marriage, finances, and parenting. One is not more important than the other. Yet, a man must be the leader. A man must make the hard decision even after he and his wife have counseled each other. A man must be the protector. Finally, a man is willing to be the final disciplinarian when children disobey the wishes of the mother.

What is a man? Psychologists over-think it like most things; nonetheless, I'm sure if you ask, you can receive a professional answer which you can ignore. However, in your heart-of-hearts you may still feel empty.

Why is that? –Because you *feel* it. You may know what I'm talking about. Does something feel wrong? Do you feel less than whole? Are you unsatisfied with your life and the unmanly status our culture has indoctrinated you into? Do you feel your soul scream deep inside as you desperately struggle to reclaim ... your manhood?

So, what is it you need? It's simple. You need what every man needs to feel whole and relevant: *Dominion.*

A man that has dominion over his life feels whole. He has peace. There is harmony in the home, in his marriage, and with his children. He has control over his finances and is not overburdened with debt.

A man with dominion has a strong relationship with God. He has no shame for it, and boldly declares it.

A man with dominion over his life builds a hedge of protection around the perimeter of his house and will die defending it. He chooses to lead and protect his family.

In short, he's a man.

Discussed in the chapters of this book are examples of shameful mistakes that I, and others, have made. I felt it was important to bring them to light. As men, we hope to *grow* from our mistakes, and commit to not making them again. We want to become better men that what we already are. Sometimes we fail, but we cannot give up.

So, what do I think is the secret ingredient? It's *Faith.* It's submission to a higher power other than you.

If this offends you, then that's why you need to read this book. Your pride is clearly an impediment you are dealing with.

I make no apologies for being a Christian man. I boldly declare it. Jesus is Lord. I will not strictly use a Christian platform to discuss what comes next in this book, but in full disclosure, you, as the reader, need to know He is my source.

Thank you for reading this work; and now that you have this knowledge, let's move forward. –Or, you can put down this book. The choice is yours. I hope you choose to read on.

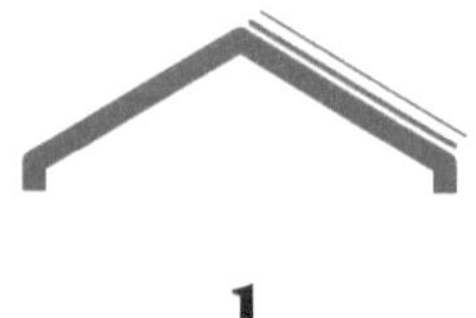

# 1

# Real Men Don't Want to Live with Their Parents

"Therefore, a man shall leave his father and his mother and hold fast to his wife, and they shall become one flesh."
Gen 2:24, ESV

Hopefully, we all love our parents. I certainly love mine. But there comes a time when a man has to step forward into the great unknown.

We were never designed to forever hold the skirt tails of our mother nor the hand of our father. Once we have fully grown, and are capable of self-care, then it is our obligation to leave the nest. As men, we do not have the right to expect our parents to forever care for us. It is not their responsibility.

In 1990, I graduated from high school with no plan. I was not motivated in regards to the future (not the best tactic). For four or five months I continued working part-time in a restaurant wondering what I was going to do, but I knew the free ride was over. For eighteen years, my mother and stepfather had invested their sweat, tears, and fortune into my future. They were expecting a return on their investment. What parent wouldn't? They hoped that their years of effort would pay off. –Hoped that I would become a productive member of society. They hoped that I would mature as an adult and take care of myself. All parents expect their children to take care of themselves and not constantly ask for help.

It's important to pause here for a moment and talk about asking for help from family. No one should read too much into this. There is no shame in seeking help from family or parents when it is truly needed. However, it should be clear that any help given is temporary and not a long-term expectation. Men that have midlife crises, for example, and decide to quit a job, move back in with their parents, and enroll in school fulltime because they want a new career, are being parasites.

It is not your parent's responsibility to make you happy. That's for you to manage. Figure out another plan that doesn't involve putting a burden on them.

SINCE THE FALL OF ADAM and the entrance of sin in the world, we have had to work to survive. Children *must* mature to be self-sustaining. Every bird eventually takes the first step off the precipice of the nest.

Personally, the decision to leave home and take care of myself was intimidating, however, I manned up and walked into an army recruiting station when I realized I needed to take a radical step to securing my future. Some paperwork, lengthy waiting and evaluations, and nine weeks of training later, I was a Private serving my country half-a-world away. I was homesick for quite a while and nervous about living on my own, but it needed to be done. But once the decision was made, I never looked back.

I'll tell more of this adventure in a later chapter.

After three years, I returned to the United States and decided to earn a college degree. I needed to reduce costs as much as possible, so I worked out an agreement with my sister to live with her as a college student. She was still family, however, so there were two things that made our arrangement *temporary*. First, I gave her money as often as I could and even pitched in doing work on the house when needed. Second, she knew once I was finished my education, I would leave and take care of myself. I didn't stick around and live in her basement, make excuses about needing more time, or force her to ask me to leave. I was man enough to do it without being told to do so.

I will be eternally grateful for what she did for me and know that it was a sacrifice for her. But again, it was temporary and she rightfully expected it to be so.

If a man is past the age of eighteen and not enrolled in college, vocational, or other educational training (again, temporary) and still living at home, he needs to ask himself *why*? Why am I not willing to take care of myself? Why am I still living in the same room I had when I was twelve?

Why indeed.... Time to be a man.

Today, twenty percent of men, ages twenty-five to thirty-four, are living at home with their parents.[1] Good grief!

"But you don't understand," some would argue. "I lost my job and can't find work!"

Hog wash.

You may not have the lifestyle you think you deserve, but you can still work a lower-paying job and meet you living needs.

"Not true!"

Yes, true.

**Luxuries do not equal survival.**

But aren't parents supposed to take care of their children? Yes, but not until *death do you part.*

It is a horrible tragedy to me when parents have the life sucked out of them by their children.

I personally know of a woman in her late thirties that has lived with her mother her entire life since passing the age of eighteen. Early on, she married a man that was already doing what she was doing. It was the perfect recipe for disaster.

Over the next decade, the marriage slowly decayed even though two children were added to the family. From outward appearance, all seemed well; but I could see the early signs of failure.

The first mistake was no financial discipline, and then came the hand-off. What was the hand-off? The hand off was when, as the parents, they quit raising their kids. The grandparents, or in this case the grandmother, took over. Year after year I watched as the grandparent did all the parenting while the parents stood by. Grandma would do all the running of the children, and even clean the daughter's house because she and her husband were too self-indulged to provide a healthy and clean home for their children.

The parents would occasionally take a plug at discipline, but it was to placate their own pride, not out of any genuine concern for the character development of their children. Did they love their children? Of course, they did. Did they love them enough to do the very best they could to ensure their development and character as they grew older? No, they didn't. They loved themselves more.

Once the marriage fell apart, the daughter moved in with her mother and brought the children with her. I'm sure this seemed like a good idea, but, of course it just solidified the role of the grandparent as the parent of the children, and the daughter as a vampire to her mother.

The children are much older now and have serious issues with personal conduct, self-discipline, and character. It was predictable early on.

And the father? Well, he was never a man. He never assumed leadership of his family, never organized and disciplined his family finances, and never insisted on raising his own children. In short, he left his man card at the altar.

Why was this the case? Why did he make the decisions he made, and why was he passive in his role as the father? –Because he was raised the same way and chose to do the same to his family. He never fully matured as a man so therefore didn't know how to be one. This can be overcome. Many men have done so, but the *will* to change has to be there.

When a child is forced to live with parents who love themselves more than the child, it assassinates the child's long-term character development.

SHOULDN'T I EXPECT help from my parents even if I have a low paying job?

No. That's the blunt answer. Again, be a man. If you make enough money to keep a roof over your head (not a mansion), and food in your gut (not daily cuisine), then you have no right to ask for help. Even if you are homeless and need shelter, thus returning to your parent's home, then you still need to realize it is temporary. You should respect this and work diligently to improve your situation to get back on your own feet, and then leave with an attitude of gratitude.

COMPARE THE MODERN "man" with those from the past. In 1930, life was tough because of the 1929 market crash and the following depression. I mean it was *really* tough. At one point, the unemployment rate was almost 26%.[2] In addition, there were no social programs to help. If you had no job, you had no money. Similarly, hundreds of thousands of people, whole families, were ripped from the heartland of America when the Dust Bowl destroyed their farmland and way of life. You were either a man, or you died. There were no other options. Food was in such short supply people were starving to death. many would scour the fields or hills for young dandelion shoots in the early spring. –Oftentimes kicking over remnants of snow to get to the new shoots growing in the soil. Children would take turns eating every other day. Folks who lived in the cities would wait for hours in food lines only to find out the food was gone by the time they reached the front of the line. Living during the depression was very, very, hard and most people resented being forced to depend on others. There was a perceived stigma of shame in doing so. Nonetheless, some social relief came in the form of financial help to states from the federal government, but not until 1932.[3]

Yet, when the nightmare of the Depression finally ended, grown men tightened the belts and went back to work. Was every man the model of self-sufficiency? Of course not, but it was deemed socially disgraceful if you did not work and was able to.

Today, dependence on others seems fashionable. Get out of your parents' basement. Earn your own bread. Be a man.

One exception needs to be addressed. When caring for an elderly or aging parent, and you need to live jointly, then that is perfectly acceptable. In no way is needing to care for a parent unmanly. In fact, it is manly. Ailing parents need to know we are there for their final years, and frankly, it's a small price to pay for the decades of care they provided you.

# 2

# To a Real Man, Life is More Important Than Gaming

"Finally, brothers, whatever is true, whatever is honorable, whatever is just, whatever is pure, whatever is lovely, whatever is commendable, if there is any excellence, if there is anything worthy of praise, think about these things."
Philippians 4:8 ESV

There is nothing sadder than a thirty-year-old that gets excited over a new video game. Are you kidding me!?

Some time ago, I was sitting in a doctor's office with my son Ryan wishing I had a shotgun to shoot the wall-mounted television. A reality show was airing that portrayed a grown man, who looked to be in his middle thirties, throwing a fit at a game store because there was something wrong with the video game he had purchased. The man was *literally* throwing a fit. The only thing he did not do was roll on the floor and beat it with his fists. His behavior was deplorable and he had to be escorted out of the store by security. All I could think was how our ancestors would react to such an act of immaturity. Alexander Hamilton was an aide-de-camp to General George Washington and a Colonel in the Continental Army in his early twenties!

If I had to identify the one thing that I believed was killing manhood in America, it'd be *entertainment addiction*. The biggest culprit, sports, can be addictive. When taken to extreme, digital or reality, sports can become a religion. It consumes every aspect of a man's identity and provides a validation for manhood. This false sense of identity is doomed to fail since our only validation can be found through the Word of God.

Are sports bad for the development of men? Of course not. Sports are a great tool for honing a young man's physical abilities and to compete against others. Sports are fantastic for eye-hand coordination and speed. Sports teach us to work together as a team to accomplish a singular goal. Any youth physically able to participate in sports should do so wholeheartedly! But, if you are thirty-five years old and spend more time in a football jersey living an avatar life than talking to your wife or spending time with your children, you have issues. If you spend more time arranging for a weekend football get-away, than you do managing your finances, then you have issues. If you believe that football or basketball is more important than spending time playing Legos with your children, that's right, you have issues.

What I am saying is this: Real men enjoy sports *because* its quality time with their son or daughter, or a rare moment of leisure time; *not* because it's the center of their life. Real men enjoy sports as a moment of relaxation when all other life requirements have been met; not calling in sick from work because they would rather watch or attend a game. Real men don't obsess over what teams are playing during March Madness, they'd rather read a storybook to their children before bedtime. Real men don't exhaust mental energy memorizing useless sports facts just to impress their friends with their pseudo man-ness, rather, they spend time fixing the leaking faucet that needs repaired.

**A real man will discipline himself to attend to the needs of his family before pursing his own interests.**

Other signs that a man is living in a false world is the "man cave." Don't you love this? The man cave is seen as the ultimate pinnacle to manliness. I've seen man caves that look like something out of Willy Wonka's Chocolate Factory. It's mindboggling. –Large screen televisions that cover an entire wall. Oversized lounge chairs. Full service bars for drinks. Refrigerators that hold every type of food a man could want; and video games stacked by the dozens in storage racks. If you're really serious, pool and hockey tables complete the room.

Whole social events are organized around the man cave. Friends are invited over so that the king of the man cave can brag about how deep his addiction really is.

In rural West Virginia, where I live, entertainment addiction is almost as serious as drug addiction. Families, live in shanty homes or trailers that have one or two satellite dishes. Tarps weighed down with tires cover roofs that need replaced, but the new car looks nice. Plywood covers the windows, but three or four ATVs are parked in the driveway.

**Poverty does not equal uncleanliness or ignorance. Uncleanliness and ignorance are by choice.**

Of course, there are exceptions. Some of the poorest people I know keep clean and tidy homes and are raising their children admirably. None of them drive new cars, and most have no television in the home, but they make wise choices with the resources they have and put entertainment on the back burner.

Entertainment addiction can take other forms, but again, is your family more important? What is the entertainment addiction in your life? What is distracting you from being a man?

So how do I know if I'm being a man or living in a fantasy world? Easy. Are you doing anything that is before God, your marriage, or your children? If so, you are allowing something to seriously compromise your manliness. Entertainment addiction is usually the culprit, but it could be other things not so noticeable. Sometimes a man will pursue new toys. –A bigger and better four-wheeler, a new fishing boat, a new camper, new hunting rifle, etc. These things, which may not be needed, can put serious financial strain on a family.

A new iPhone to replace the old one, a new tablet or computer because the ones you have are not the latest models. Or, perhaps a new car every year whether you need one or not?

Many years ago when my wife and I married, and eventually had our first child a little over a year later, we were living on a very tight budget. I was a school teacher.

We were paying rent on a small cottage house in the rural area of Morganton, NC; where I taught at a middle school as a special education and history teacher. Things were very tight and paying bills and keeping food in the house was always a struggle. We owned a used car that was pretty old, but running. –But that wasn't good enough for me. I had to have a Jeep Wrangler. I had always wanted one and was obsessed with having it. I let the desire overwhelm my good judgement and bought a used one (entertainment addiction) without consulting my wife. She wasn't happy, to say the least.

We really couldn't afford the Jeep, but I didn't let that stop me from buying it. I had what *I* wanted, even though it was the wrong decision for my family's needs financially. I checked my man card at the dealership and took my new toy home like a twelve-year-old. Eventually, the Jeep was repossessed, but that is a story for later....

**Entertainment addiction can affect the entire family; though it's ultimately the parents' responsibility.**

Several years ago, I took my family to Disney World. It wasn't an impulsive decision. We had planned to do so for some time, however, we refused to do so if it caused financial strain on the family. So, when the opportunity came which provided an affordable trip –without creating a burden of debt- we made the decision to finally go. Our trip proved to be a magical and fun experience for our children. They had an amazing time. But not all families share the same experience.

On the second day of our trip, we paused midday for a meal. We chose a place to eat, ordered our food, and sat down.

Though my children didn't notice, I could overhear the conversation of a family next to us. The children were complaining about the food they were eating as it wasn't what they wanted. The parents sharply replied, "It's what we can afford."

"Can we stay another day?" the youngest child of two asked.

"No," the Father replied glumly. "I have to get back to work."

What I noticed, that the children didn't, was the look between the parents. It was the look of: *We're out of money. –Time to go home.*

I don't know for certain that this was the case, but it proves a point:

**Impulsive and emotional decisions cause undue hardship.**

Most likely the family borrowed money for a vacation. This is all too common. Entertainment addiction consumes the family and the parents make poor decisions to appease their children.

Choosing debt over sound financial decisions is not being a man. Of course, children do not understand this. However, the inability to afford certain things in life can also be a teaching opportunity for your children. This is what my wife and I chose to do. –And because we waited to take a vacation when we could afford it, we had an amazing and enjoyable time doing so.

**Entertainment must be a cash funded commodity.**

Managing entertainment addiction is not an insurmountable problem if you are willing to change. A close examination of your life activities will yield the answer of where you are. Are you following God first, honoring your marriage second, and caring for your children and home third? If not, eliminate something in your life that is keeping you from doing so. Beneficially, you will see your stress and anxiety greatly reduced, and the happiness of your family greatly increased.

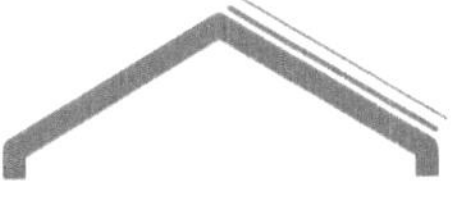

# 3

# Real Men Keep Their Word and Lead by Example

"Behold, I am with you and will keep you wherever you go, and will bring you back to this land. For I will not leave you until I have done what I have promised you."
Genesis 28:15, ESV

The words "I promise" are forbidden in my house. They are forbidden *unless* you absolutely mean it and will not violate your *word* for any reason. Other than life or limb, I cannot think of any reason for a real man to break a promise.

As a man, your word is the most important possession you have. It says everything about the man you are, and the type of man others want to be around. A man's word means something. It's a contract between one man and another. Nothing is more distasteful to a man than when someone cannot keep his word. It proves that you are not a man and that you are less than worthy of the title.

From the beginning, man's word has always represented power. God himself used the power of His Word and declared, "Let there be light."[4] There is nothing about His Word that isn't taken seriously. Why should we do any less?

Giving your word is simply honoring your commitments. This is a foreign concept in the fast-food electronic society we now live in; and I believe it is the source of why we have so much chaos in our lives as men.

An example of this is simple to demonstrate.

Occasionally, I will try to schedule time with my family. Though I love them all, they oftentimes seem to have no control of their lives. For example, a simple call trying to schedule an event two or three months ahead of time seems to illicit the same response: "Well, we'll have to see what's going on. Let me get back to you."

This is a grossly canned response. And the question is: Are you really so out-of-control of your life that you cannot make a commitment that far in advance? Is this not what calendars are for? When someone tells you "I'll have to see what's going on," it's rude. It's certainly ok to say "I'm not home so let me check my work schedule or my calendar to make sure I haven't planned anything." Or, "I need to ask my spouse in case he or she scheduled something. Can you call me this evening?" But simply stating "let's see what happens" clearly says my time is not important to you, nor do you wish to spend time with me.

Or, even worse, a flimsy commitment is made, but when the time comes, suddenly, "I can't make it."

Don't make flimsy commitments. Either do, or don't. If I can't, then I simply say, "I can't commit to that right now. Can we do it some other time when we both are free?" This shows that you respect the time of others and that you appreciate their willingness to want to spend time with you.

**Real men know that giving, and keeping, your word takes commitment and sacrifice.**

Keeping your word is often very difficult, but no matter what, as a man, I make sure that I do so. If I commit to going to a birthday party or dinner engagement, you can take it to the bank that I'll be there. If I accept a wedding invitation, I'll be there.

A few years ago, I was invited to a wedding by a fellow Soldier who sent me an invitation. I spoke to my wife about it; she agreed we could attend and that it would be nice. It was not local to us, but within a reasonable distance. I accepted the invitation.

Once we arrived, we immediately appreciated the location for the ceremony. The church chosen was an old one room church built in the late 1800's. The pews had been decorated nicely with ribbon and flowers while the day was sunny and mild as early spring often is.

We sat on the groom's side of the church, and not long after, the ceremony began. My colleague appeared in full dress uniform while the bride wore a long gown of white. The ceremony went well and the newlywed couple embraced with a kiss.

Once the congregation rose to leave, my colleague came over and warmly shook my hand.

"Thanks for coming! Wasn't sure you'd make it!"

"Why wouldn't I make it?" I asked puzzled.

"Well," he replied looking over my shoulder, "not many in my family showed up.

I smiled slightly and didn't respond. I hadn't realized how bare the pews were on the groom side until he had pointed it out.

What bothered me the most was the fact that his own family had "committed" to come to his wedding, but failed to honor their promise. –They couldn't keep their word. It was mind-boggling to me. Even if I had to rent a car to attend his wedding, I would have done so. If I had to take a vacation day from work, I would have done so. Why? –Because I gave him *my word* that I would be there!

As the wedding was wrapping up, my friend approached me and said, "Well, we're having a wedding reception over at the American Legion. I know you got a way to travel back home, but if you want to come for a few minutes, we'll have food!"

We had already planned on coming," I said smiling. "Your invitation said reception following immediately after, did it not?" I teased.

My colleague momentarily sputtered, and then nodded briskly. "You bet! I just didn't think you'd be able to stay."

"Well, I gave you my word that I'd attend your wedding, so that's what I'm here to do," I assured him patting him on the back.

Sadly, the crowd from the church to the reception had thinned by nearly half. His other guests must have had something more important to do....

In an age of technology, it becomes more and more important as men to honor our word. With instant communication and gratification, we need to slow down and ensure that our word is not being compromised. This will often involve long hours with others when we are pressed to do other things. Do it anyway. More often than not, you will realize the time committed was well worth it.

Keeping your word also means the small stuff. If you promise your wife to empty the dishwasher, do it. If you promise your kids that you will throw some ball with them, you better follow through. Nothing will damage the trust and faith of a child more than breaking promises over and over again. If you make a promise to members of your community or church, then you demonstrate your integrity based on whether or not you can keep your word.

Some time ago, my church purchased a building to renovate. As part of that remodel, the Pastor and an Elder asked if I could build a set of shelves for the nursery.

"Sure," I replied. "When do you need them?"

"Well," the Elder replied, "we're still working on the building, so whenever, really."

I'm paraphrasing our conversation, but soon, I had the shelves ready; and once the nursery was completed, it served its purpose.

The point being, I gave my word, and I followed through on that promise. I didn't make excuses. Did it take time that I could have put elsewhere? Sure. But it was a labor of love, and it will please me to see the shelves being used for years to come.

Sometimes we are tested by others who may not know us that well; and whether we know it or not, we're being watched. People need to know if you're reliable. It's so rare in the modern era that we need to look to the past for examples.

In the book, *The Go-Getter*,[5] Bill Peck demonstrated his absolute refusal to break his word.

Maimed, and missing one arm from the First World War, he called on a lumber company for a sales job.

Reluctant to hire him, a senior manager took the gamble and agreed to let him prove his mettle.

Not long after, Mr. Peck demonstrated that he could outsell timber more than any other salesman. Soon he was being considered for an overseas position, but to be sure he could fully be trusted, he had to be tested. –He had to "deliver a blue vase."

The test involved the following: The Senior managers dear friend was a collector of vases, and had an anniversary coming shortly. A particular pretty blue vase was in the shop window of a downtown store. Mr. Peck was to retrieve the vase, drop it in the mail by that afternoon, so that it would reach the friend prior to her anniversary. If he did not get it mailed by that afternoon, then she would not receive the vase in time.

Unbeknownst to Mr. Peck, he was being setup. It was Friday, and the store would not reopen until Monday.

The book goes on to detail the extreme measures that Mr. Peck endured to get the vase. It would put any modern man to shame. But, he got the job done.

After some time to let him cool, his Senior manager finally confessed as to why he was given the *Degree of the Blue Vase*. He had a major promotion in mind for him and needed to see of if he could handle the job and be trusted with absolute loyalty. –He was to be given a promotion to lead an entire division at an overseas office.

The intent of sharing this part of the book, which is wholly worth the read, is one statement made by Mr. Bill Peck when he was asked why he just didn't quit:

"Because my Brigadier [General] had a motto: It shall be done. When we were given an order to occupy a certain territory, we knew it would be done, or we would die trying."

In the statement "It shall be done," there are four simple words that have a greater power than the physical strength of any man. It is an unbreakable bond of a promise, and that no matter what, no matter the circumstances; your word will be honored.

**Real men know that a promise means: *It Shall Be Done!***

Men like Mr. Peck used to be common. Today, he is an endangered species.

The need to be a man of character seems to have dwindled from American society. I attribute this to disengagement from father's who spend most of their time in the pursuit of entertainment addiction and instant gratification.

As men we need to work diligently to preserve our commitment to our word. It is the foundation to who we are as men. Without the bond of our word, and thereby the promises we make, we are shallow excuses for what a man should be. We have no substance, and are an irritation to those that we associate with. We are seen as unreliable and untrustworthy. It affects all areas of our lives; relationships with our wives, our children, our friends, and our work colleagues.

Everyone respects a man that honors his word above all else. People are drawn to him like a magnet. Such men become the leaders of the world, as others wonder in envy why they are successful.

Thankfully, the key to honorable living is not complicated; fore men are simple creations. We need only do two things in this life: Obey God's Word, and honor our own.

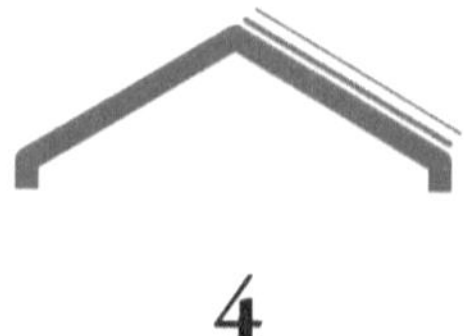

# 4

# Real Men Respect and Pursue the Art of Compromise

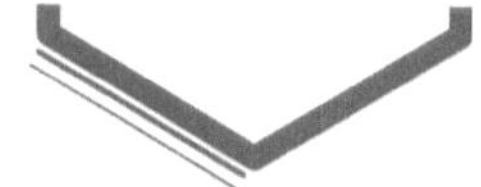

"When a man's ways please the Lord, he makes even his enemies to be at peace with him."
Proverbs 16:7, ESV

It is no mystery that our country has never been more politically divided. Yet I simply cannot believe that Americans have given up on solving our problems; or that we will simply continue to focus our efforts on treating our ailments yet never trying to cure them. I cannot believe we no longer have the ability to compromise when governing. –I can't believe any of it. Yet, we fight viciously and vindictively. Much of our squabble also plays out in view of the world. –Not with civility and respect for each other, but with contempt and loathing. It's not healthy for a Republic to act this way.

Much of the contention between Americans rests on the view of our civil rights. Whether Liberal or Conservative, the key is to *respect* the opinions of those you disagree with and seek common ground with civility.

Respect and civility used to be largely common in government, yet somehow, this has been lost. For example, in my opinion,

Abraham Lincoln was a master statesman. He never lost his commitment to civility and respect. Even at times when he vehemently disagreed, he always remembered to be civil and mindful that disagreement did not have to mean disparagement. He was a real man.

**Real men don't disparage others if they disagree with them.**

While running for his party nomination in 1860, Abraham Lincoln gave a speech, known as the "Copper Union Address," that shows the remarkable wisdom that he always maintained when dealing with people. He began his speech with an acknowledgement of Southerners. Also, keep in mind that tensions were high as civil war was looming; beginning with South Carolina succeeding later that same year after his eventual election to the presidency: "I consider that in the general qualities of reason and justice you [Southerners] are not inferior to any people."

Respect. – Plain and simple.

Fast forward to any hotly contested topic of today and the dialogue is somewhat ... shall we say ... colorful?

Let's go with guns.

To give full disclosure, I am a supporter of guns rights. I believe that our forefathers exercised great wisdom in guaranteeing this right to all citizens for our protection against an oppressive government. Nonetheless, to summarily dismiss the concerns of gun violence is equal to putting your head in the sand.

**Real men are open to dialogue at all times and willing to hear the concerns of others.**

Because we have a great deal of gun violence, it is easy to look at the object of cause, guns, and want to just remove them from the equation. Nonetheless, it is critical to remember that guns are simply tools. They have no tangible fault on their own. It would be equivalent to banning shovels because they are the cause of too many ditches being dug. Tools are just tools. The real cause of gun violence is the people wielding them unjustly. So, from a conservative view, we have a social deficiency.

Gun control supporters feel that guns have no further use on our society; or that we need to put tougher restrictions on their availability, use, or just eliminate them altogether.

Because this is a passionate issue for both views, compromise is needed. As a conservative, I would argue that, to relieve our society of those that feel life has no value (violent gun offenders), we need to put more emphasis on saving the family unit and work harder to decrease single parent households. It is generally accepted that broken homes have greater incidents of socially unstable youth. Additionally, a greater involvement of parents eliminating violent media from the cultural diet of their children would help alleviate the misconception that life has no value. There is no argument that a healthy family environment generally results in healthy, socially stable, children.

Further, we need to involve media outlets (movie, television, and gaming producers) and social platforms to put an emphasis on teaching the value of life and the value of respecting others. Violence needs to be addressed in the propaganda directed to youth. Gun use and safety needs to be part of the dialogue in communities, and I'd also like to see the same added to the public school curriculum. There should be no stigma to teaching gun safety and use to a society that is constitutionally guaranteed the right to bear arms.

This is a long-term plan to addressing the social deficiencies we have with guns, but as some of you are thinking, what about now?

Because I know that I cannot convince everyone that guns are not the issue, then compromises are needed. For example, as a gun owner and supporter, I would be willing to support an increased focus on the illegal trafficking of guns and stiffer legal penalties; and I would be willing to increase the liability of those who neglectfully allow their personally owned guns to be used for mass violence. –A secure gun is a safe gun.

**A real man understands that his view is not the only view.**

OBVIOUSLY, THERE ARE many disputed social topics that Americans and their politicians are polarized over; gun control is just one.

Dialogue over toxic issues can also become heated. This is sometimes an unavoidable fact since we are all human. Nonetheless, mature adults accept this fact and move forward without succumbing to their anger.

Abraham Lincoln was also very good at controlling his anger. To refrain himself from disparaging someone under his command as Commander-in-chief, or someone that was a political opponent or colleague, he would compose "hot letters" and then put them away for a time. He would then later pull them out and write on them: "Never sent, never signed."

This is far from what is now considered wise political practice!

Americans used to try to temper their tongue and remain civil. Now, it's seen as normal to instantly lash out with verbal vomit when angry on social media platforms. –And I would argue that this has become the single most inflammatory source of discontent within our society causing extreme polarity in our communities.

**Real men temper their anger and remain civil when seeking compromise.**

COMPROMISE CAN OFTEN be viewed as a dirty word. However, compromise is only a weakness if your core beliefs are threatened and you capitulate against them. Nonetheless, to find common ground with someone, you start right there: what ground do you have in common? Once these commonalities are determined, then dialogue and agreement can eventually be reached.

In 2016, Donald Trump won the Presidency of the United States. At the time, I'd never seen such an immature response of Americans. Violent riots erupted in several major U.S. cities because Hilary Clinton, the Democratic nominee, did not win. Yet, in a republic that elects a President every four years, someone always loses. This has been the case since the beginning. What exactly were Americans expecting?

The majority of rioters were young Americans. If we take a closer look at *why* they are protesting, we can see how they have been groomed socially to believe that "every player on the team gets a trophy." They honestly believed that people with other points of views or opinions did not have the right to vote in opposition to their own views. This is a disturbing, and highly probable fact, that taking civics from mainstream public education was a gross mistake. Ignorance of our political process and how to be tolerant of it is a serious deficiency in young Americans.

**A real man respects the rule of law and his system of government.**

AT THE CORE OF BEING socially stable and proficient at compromise, is learning the art of living with your neighbors and other people in the community. When in close proximity to other people, you are forced to tolerate each other. This can be extremely difficult in some cases, but nonetheless, compromise is preferable to discontent or even violence.

When my wife and I first moved back to West Virginia in 2010, we met our neighbors very quickly. Soon, one neighbor moved out and a new family moved in. They had children of their own. –Two older girls and a young boy about my son's age.

As time passed, my wife and I found ourselves offending our neighbors time and time again. To this day we're still not quite sure what we were doing, but it was evident that they were not happy since the relationship always seemed to be in a cycle of "this week they like us, next week not so much."

One on occasion, it blew up into an argument right at the property line. My father-in-law, who lived with us, was nose to nose with Mrs. Neighbor, and for a moment, I thought it was going to go to blows. I intervened and finally cooler heads prevailed. The result was both families set up a defense perimeter. Because I was rarely home and always working, I would listen to my wife tell how, even when outside, nobody would even talk to each other. This was relatively easy to do since our houses were well apart, and there was no real reason to walk past one another.

One day, I was outside chopping wood and noticed my son, who was six at the time, standing at the property line staring at the neighbor's son; who was also standing on the property line staring back. One thing that all the adults had missed was how our children set a better example than the rest of us. They didn't care about trivial squabbles and dumb adult arguments. They just missed each other and playing together. They only wanted to go back to being buddies like they were before; because, as part of the "war," they were not permitted to "associate with the enemy." For the first time, I was being shown how to be real man by my six-year-old son. I had failed to heal the divide.

**A real man will not ignore his responsibilities of reconciliation.**

I knew that I had to do something, yet, just walking to the front door would probably not get the result I was looking for. My attempt at reconciliation may be misconstrued as criticism before I could fully explain my intent. So, instead, I elected to write a letter.

There is much to be said for the simple letter; as Lincoln proved. I believe it is an art of communication that desperately needs revived. Writing a letter, in your own handwriting does several things. First, it shows that you truly care since you took the time to physically write instead of texting or typing. The very act of writing takes time and commitment. Second, and most importantly, you cannot be interrupted when speaking by the person reading your letter. –Thereby negating the possibility of an argument starting.

Taking time to think out exactly what to say, I began a carefully written letter that was well thought out and to the point. I wrote a letter expressing my genuine sorrow and regret that our families could not live more peacefully with each other. I also added apologies for any offense we may have committed and honestly asked what we could do to improve our relationship. Lastly, I detailed how our children were missing the rich reward of their friendship and did not deserve our anger against them.

I walked that letter over to their front door and then went home feeling much better.

A couple days went by and nothing was ever said about the letter. Then, the next weekend, Ethan came running into the house very excited. "Mom, Dad! Bobby[6] wants to play! His mom said we could play! Can we!?"

My wife and I glanced at each other, and then I looked back at Ethan. "Sure, Son. Go ahead, but remember your manners."

He bolted out of the house with the biggest grin ever.

I walked outside on the deck and looked over to the neighbor's house. There standing on the deck was Bobby's parents. I waved. They waved back. *It's not much,* I thought to myself, smiling. *But it's a start!*

As the weeks and months went by, our relationship blossomed into one of mutual respect and friendship. We truly got to know them well, and I was grateful we made the effort to change.

They have moved away now, but we still remain in touch over social media. My wife and I can say we honestly miss them and was grateful that we got to finally know them for who they truly were.

**A real man persistently works at relationships with other people even when it seems insurmountable.**

True respect cannot blossom without compromise. You are not always right. Be a real man and get over it. Consistently work at being civil to others and be willing to listen whether you agree or not. The most offensive thing you can do is immediately disagree with a statement given in all sincerity. There is no conversational law requiring you to immediately respond to any question or statement offered by another. Show maturity and respect for others by being a real man and give it some thought. It's okay to say "Let me give that some thought." When you are ready and have researched the facts, calmly and respectfully respond. Never do so with hostility. Be a real man and master the art of compromise and respect.

# 5

# Real Men are Bullet Proof Against Toxic People

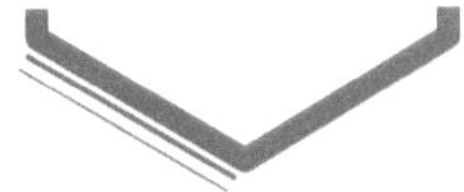

"The wise lay up knowledge, but the mouth of a fool brings ruin near."
Proverbs 10:14, ESV

It's important to say that we are all children of God. However, there may be times in your life that you will need to separate yourself from those who are toxic to you.

We all know the type: People who refuse to change for the better. People who believe that there is nothing wrong with them, and blame the world for never understanding. These same people ignore the sound advice of their loved ones and continue down destructive paths.

Toxic people believe that their desires, wants, and needs supersede all others; and genuinely get offended when confronted about it. They suck the life-blood from your soul and consume your time.

Toxic people believe that no one is as important as they are. Surely, they have loved ones they care deeply about, but only behind themselves.

Toxic people demand that all the attention is constantly on them. They get angry and throw tantrums when this is not the case. The tantrums may be in adult form, such as angry outbursts, yelling, or accusations of supposed wrong doing; or they are more sinister in nature and try to guilt you into submission. Other tantrums are more organized and violent in nature when tied together with groups of people recruited to their cause. These are called riots.

A real man has no patience for such folly. In fact, a real man refuses to allow toxic people to rule him or to influence him negatively.

## A real man separates himself from the toxic leeches that drain away life-blood.

The greatest tool a toxic person has is being your relative. They use this blood-connection to wedge themselves into your life. This blood-connection also allows them to guilt their way into getting what they want. It is unfortunate and sad, but true. And oftentimes, the victim says nothing because "we're kin, after all."

Whether you have a family member or friend poisoning your well, you must be brave enough to confront it. If you do not, your life will never grow and flourish as it was meant to.

Many years ago, after completing my first military tour, I returned home. As mentioned before, I was intent on going to school and continuing my education. Yet the transition was strangely difficult.

Once settled in temporarily with family, I started to run into old high school friends. Relationships that had faded once again were renewed. At first, I thought this would be nice, but then I soon learned things were different.

One very good friend, in particular, I reconnected with because of our strong friendship in high school. It became apparent to me that he had done literally nothing for three years. He was still my friend, but I was saddened that he had not moved beyond high school. He was proud of the fact that he still "visited the band room" from time to time to say hello to our old band director (We both were band students). However, it must have been odd to current high school students, who remembered him less and less as time progressed, that he was coming to the high school.[7]

To a real man, this is disheartening. It goes against the grain of the soul to be stuck in the past while not moving towards the future.

**Real men always strive to the future while still honoring the past.**

As time passed, my good friend tried harder and harder to pull me into the bad habits that we both pursued in high school. –Partying, drinking, and general idleness that I simply no longer had an interest in. As a result, I had to quit associating with my friend because of his unwillingness to change and to move on as an adult. Sometimes removing yourself from toxic people can be a painful process. However, failure to do so can result in catastrophic results.

After almost three years in the Army, I was determined to complete my college degree. If I'd reverted back to old habits, more than likely my future would have been drastically altered.

As a parent, you have to be aware that toxic people can drastically affect the development of your children. Do you have children? Do you protect who they spend their time with? I'm not speaking of allowing your children to spend time with dangerous people, but rather, people that are a bad influence on their character development.[8]

I remember years ago when it became apparent that a relative would be around my children on a daily basis. The relative had a very bad habit of swearing constantly. Because so, I was forced to confront my relative and boldly state that swearing was not permissible around my children. This did not go so well at first, but when it was clear that I was not going to yield on the issue, the relative finally consented and respected my wishes on the matter. I was glad that it worked out. However, if it hadn't, I would have done whatever necessary to remove the relative from the presence of my children.

**Real men are willing to remove toxic influences from the presence of their families.**

Toxic people are dangerous. –Especially when they argue, "a real friend would accept me for who I am."

The deepest and most insidious tool used by toxic people is your heart. This tactic is so devious that few can escape its attack. You need to politely but rightfully rebuke the offender. If not, it's like a black hole with insatiable hunger. You are slowly torn apart as forces that seem beyond your control spin your life into chaos. Though you feel compelled to keep forgiving, you must not if he or she refuses to apologize and cease the toxic behavior. The risk to you or your family is too great.

A very personal experience illustrates this danger.

My initial enlistment in the Army had a significant impact on me. It goes without saying that the best part of the military experience is the long-lasting friendships you develop. Your battle buddies become brothers. –Family. You have a bond so close that you are willing to die for them. It's why being in uniform is so special to many people.

One particular brother-in-arms was Tyler.[9]

I remember meeting Tyler for the first time. He was a Texan with a thick southern dialect. I immediately took a liking to him since we both had a dialect that made us the brunt of many well-rounded jokes. Tyler was hotheaded and always let his pride take him further than he could handle.

From the first day of training, we did everything together. We were in the same platoon though different squads. Whenever he got "smoked," I was on the ground with him taking my share of the blame. –Not because I did anything wrong, but because that was my brother; and when he got smoked, I got smoked. He did the same for me. It didn't matter. Once when all us recruits had our belongings thrown out the windows for a barracks inspection at 3:00 AM, and then were summarily marched out to the sand pit in our underwear and boots in the rain to get smoked for our "sins," he purposefully muscled his way to the front of the formation to stand by me.

"What are you doing?" I asked trying to see through the rain running down my face.

"If I'm going to get smoked, I want to be with my battle buddy!" he smiled.

"You look ridiculous in boots and underwear," I chided.

"Look who's talking Hog Boy!"[10]

For over two hours we rolled in that sand, and no matter what, we didn't care. It was all good.

AFTER OUR INFANTRY training, we both had the good fortune of getting the same assignment: Vilseck, Germany.

"Dude, this is awesome," I said slapping him on the back. "Once we get over there, we need to try to get in the same platoon again."

"You know it," he smiled. "See you after R&R."

We parted ways, finished our short leave, and then met back up at our new assignment overseas.

We managed to again get in the same platoon, and at first things went well. Yet as time went by, and months turned to years, Tyler started to drink heavily.

Pausing the story for a moment, it's important to clarify that drinking alcohol is not a sin. Some argue that, if you abstain, you can lead a morally clean life. Biblically, that is simply not the case. It's healthier, but there is no moral equivalence to drinking or not drinking. What God's Word *is* clear on is that he prohibits drunkenness.[11] It also prohibits you from leading your brother or sister to sin.[12] So, you should not present alcohol to anyone struggling with or recovering from a drinking problem. In addition, if you personally cannot control how much alcohol you drink, you've crossed the line. Be wise and stay away from it.

At first, I went along with Tyler; because that's what battle buddies do. Though I pressed him hard to slow down, we always ended up back in the bar; and on more than one occasion, ending up at the wrong end of a fist! It was common for him to report for duty after a weekend pass with a swollen lip or the hint of a shiner. –Then came the day he had one drink to many and the consequences were severe.

It was a typical week of training that ended up with the typical plans for the weekend. But, this time, Tyler surprised me.

"You want to go hang out a party this weekend? –Being the 4^{th} of July and all, one of the other Soldier's and his wife are having a party."

I thought, *sure, why not? Following him to the bar was getting old. –Should be good since it's a married couple's house on base.*

"Okay, let's do it," I replied feeling reassured.

After we were released from duty, we changed and left for the party.

The party was fun and there were lots of people from our Company there. I was grateful for the invitation since I had been away from home for over a year. It was nice to be in a home where I could see a family again; even if it wasn't mine.

As the night progressed, things remained pleasant and uneventful. Then, someone hollered, "There's a fight starting on the patio outside!"

I ran with the crowd and found Tyler at the center of attention. Drunken and slovenly trying to put together a coherent sentence, he was threatening a very large and imposing soldier. I'd never met the other soldier before, but I could tell Tyler was way out of his league. –And at the moment, the other very large soldier was losing his patience.

"Whoa, bud," I said immediately throwing myself between him and the soldier that was about to tear him in half. "We're guests in someone else's house, and you are about to do something you don't want to do."

"You stay out of it!" Tyler replied, slobbering all over me. "I got this! I'll eat this guy for breakfast!"

The other soldier, to his credit, did not seem to be drinking and was keeping his cool.

"Tyler, you need to cool down."

"Whatever!" he relented, storming off. "I need another drink."

I couldn't disagree more, but if he was willing to let it go, I was willing to give him time to cool off. I went back inside to enjoy the party.

"Fight, fight, fight!" I heard erupt outside. I knew immediately that Tyler had circled around. I should have guessed that was what he'd do. *Stupid!*

I went back outside, but I was too late. Very big soldier had already given Tyler a very bloody lip, and Tyler was moving in for more.

Trying again, I jumped in the middle.

"Tyler, knock it off! You're drunk!"

"Stay out of it," he said trying to push me aside. He was so drunk he missed me completely and nearly fell down.

"You better get him outta here," very big soldier warned. "I've had enough of his mouth!"

"I'll tell *you* when *I'm* finished talking, boy!" Tyler yelled.

Tyler took another swing, and very big soldier dodged easily. I jumped in between just as very big soldier swung in response, but I was the one who took the punch.

My head exploded into a thousand stars and I staggered at the force of his punch. It just about knocked me cold.

I was just aware enough to see very big soldier land one more punch on Tyler. Tyler didn't stand back up. But, by that time, it was too late. Someone had already called the MP's.

ABOUT AN HOUR AND A full statement later, I sat in the brig with Tyler. He was still drunk and sleeping on the bench. It didn't matter that I had tried to stop him, I was sitting in the drunk room with him. There were bars between me and freedom; and I knew full well that I would see our Commander in the morning. There was little to no patience in the army for drunken disorderly conduct, and since Tyler had a history already, I knew the Commander would not be lenient. We were going to get the hammer.

Looking at my sleeping friend, I knew I was about to do something I would deeply regret. Nonetheless, I had to make a decision, or he would take me further down a road that I wouldn't be able to come back from.

It was going to be a long restless night for me.

THE NEXT MORNING, TYLER had sobered enough to speak coherently; even though he had a hangover of champions. The Commander still hadn't arrived, so I knew I had little time to tell him.

"Tyler, what you did was wrong," I started.

"I was drunk," he croaked out.

"Do you even know why you were fighting?" I pressed.

He didn't answer.

"Whatever the reason, I can't keep doing this with you," I said bluntly. "It's time we go our separate ways."

"What are you saying?" he chuckled. "You know it don't mean nothing. We'll be fine. The CO will get over it."

You don't remember saying that once before? –Because I remember you saying it. –On more than one occasion. I also remember you saying you'd never do it again, too."

He stared at me with bloodshot eyes. "So, what are you saying?"

"I'm saying that, if I can get out of this without getting busted in rank, I'm done with you. Find someone else to drag down with you. You're an alcoholic. Look me up when things are different."

I looked at the man who had been my battle buddy for almost two years. He was visibly shaken by my words, and I almost took them back, however, I knew that I could not. It would be up to him to change, not me.

SURVIVING TOXIC PEOPLE can sometimes be a deeply personal and painful experience. When this happens, a real man cannot "tough" his way through it. A real man realizes that, though men shouldn't be whiners or limp-wristed, they still have real feelings and vulnerabilities that only our Father God can make whole. In other words, even real men must depend on something other than themselves.

**A Real man will never allow toxic people to forever harden his heart.**

While toxic people can sometimes cut straight to your heart, they often attack with great subtlety. Instead of being an encourager, they become a destroyer. With the power of their words, they kill you with a thousand cuts.

"You don't have what it takes."

"If I were you, I'd do …"

"You weren't made to do…"

"No one in our family has ever done that."

"You shouldn't get your hopes up."

"That sounds like too much work to me."

"You're dreaming if you think you…"

"You can't do it."

"Trust me. You don't want to."

"Our family has always been failures."

"Your brothers and sisters couldn't. You can't either."

"No one will ever love you. You're lucky I even keep you around."

People who constantly speak failure in your life, though sometimes well meaning, are just as toxic as those who choose to be more blunt. These "toxic light" people are very difficult to detect. We get comfortable around them; especially if family. We begin to believe what they say as their words continually chip away our resolve to follow our dreams and goals. Be aware and on guard of the words you choose to embrace.

**Real men always filter the words of others that threaten their dreams, goals, or moral beliefs.**

Toxic people are *still* people, but ostracizing them is an absolutely critical step if you're not strong enough to keep them from destroying your life. If you believe you *are* strong enough, then with all due caution, it is perfectly sensible to have some exposure. Your example may serve as a valuable source to those who are seeking change in their lives. Most people do eventually seek harmony and happiness in their lives, and when they finally mature to accept that they are the architect of their own unhappiness, your strength and example are important to helping them commit to change.

At the end of the day, it is up to you to determine if you are in a toxic relationship. A sure test as to whether or not a relationship is healthy is if the person you are thinking about is uplifting and supportive when in conversation with you. Does he or she constantly criticize you and put you down? These simple questions are all that is needed when determining if you are in a toxic relationship.

A final point is this: know the difference between someone putting you down and criticizing, and the truth. If someone tells you that you are an alcoholic and that you need help, he or she could be the only true friend you have.

Toxic people can be found in every niche of your life. –Work, clubs, family, or mutual friends. If you know how to recognize them, then cutting them from your life is easy. Sometime subtlety is more than enough to keep unwanted influences from your life, yet, at other times, more direct confrontation may be required. Either way, the intent should be to protect yourself or your family from events that have the potential to drastically alter your future. –And if direct confrontation is needed, then do so with respect, civility, and honor God's Word. Always keep an open invitation for friendship, or forgiveness, when desired behaviors are offered.

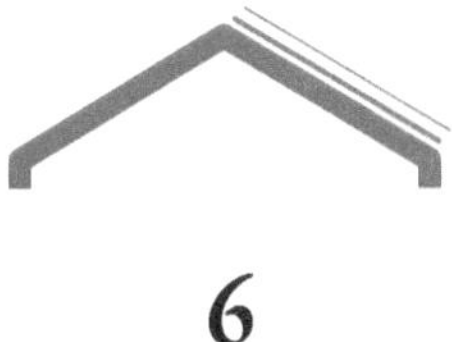

6

# Real Men Don't Require a Safe Space, and are not a Digital Narcissist

I remember an age when people used to talk. I mean really talk, not text each other from across the table. In fact, disassociation has gotten so bad that people are terrified to speak to each other. Whole generations have lost the art of just speaking.

This problem holds true even with my extended family. Moments of silence are awkward to them and they seem uncomfortable during conversation. Often, these voids in conversation are filled with staring down at their digital devices while waiting for someone to speak. They seem afraid simply to enjoy the silence or to look each other in the eyes. Or, even, worse, the digital devices become the conversation.

"Hey, I just sent you this Facebook post. You have to read this!"

"My phone is turned off," I reply. Or, "I'd rather talk to you than talk about Facebook."

This usually gets a look of guilt and a temporary reprieve from the use of their phone, but it's not long before the phone grabs their attention again.

Withdrawing into digital devices is not healthy for you. It becomes a place of comfort, a "safe space" that strips you of your ability to be socially compatible with the rest of the world. Being socially comfortable, in essence, takes practice. This used to be a normal part of becoming an adult, but since many are choosing, or have chosen, to largely skip this part of their life in favor of the digital world, it's easier to stay there than to put forth the effort of relating to people. –It's easier to stay in a safe space.

The *safe space disease* is spreading throughout our country; as many college and high school students are demanding they have access to it. Safe spaces are embraced by sociologists as a tool for peaceful dialogue, self-discovery, and freedom from anxiety and depression. It is touted as being a leap in our social progressive development. I'd argue that these are merely the symptoms of youth that have failed to learn the art of human communication and tolerance; as well as many who have suffered the modern acceptance of broken or gender-confused families. In essence, I believe we are suffering from our own social failures; directly resulting from entertainment addiction and a lethargic commitment to the family unit.

**Real men don't need safe spaces, they accept their imperfections, strive to improve them, and move on.**

I am not saying technology is completely bad. I use many social platforms and digital devices myself. What I *am* saying is that allowing media and digital devices to absolutely consume you is *not healthy!* I have learned to strictly limit myself to its exposure, and to teach the same to my children. Further, I am perfectly comfortable with *not* looking at my phone for the whole day! I can go weeks, even a whole month without checking Facebook. –And that's ok.

The benefit of this type of lifestyle is that I am very comfortable around people and enjoy conversations with them.

One excellent example of technology being beneficial is the app "Sit With Us," created by Natalie Hampton. Bullied as a student in an all-girl school, she was ostracized socially in the cafeteria every day. From the kindness of her own heart, as well as the pain she was seeking to redeem, she decided to help others instead of looking for a *Safe Space.* By doing so, she healed not only her own scars, but those of countless others. This proves that technology can be a useful and powerful tool. All across America, children that feel lonely or think they have no self-worth, can now use this tool to find others who will welcome them. Ironically, the app also does something that I've been pointing out all along: It provides the human interaction and conversation we all need to feel loved and accepted. –A wonderful reversal to the problems digital devices are creating!

**Real men are not slaves to digital devices.**

Safe spaces are misleading by their very definition. Universities are using the term to "socially enlighten" their students.

For example, at Duke University's Sanford School of Public Policy, safe spaces are identified as, "a respite from discourse that can be demeaning, antagonistic, or fraught."[13]

Seriously? How did we get to a place in our society that, grown adults, feel fraught around other people? This is the direct result of growing up in a digital world and not learning how to confront and resolve conflict with others. Adults are expected to have these basic skills already. Higher learning has evolved into daycare; where adults have the emotional maturity of preschoolers. That is not good.

Safe spaces have become gathering places to those who are confused and immature. Even though there are some who have legitimate issues with depression and anxiety, safe spaces cannot help them. Professional therapists and psychologists can. For the remaining people who demand safe spaces, you need to take a grow-up-pill. Recognize that *you* are the problem, not everyone else around you. It is your responsibility to develop a viable and a healthy self-image. Choose to embrace and emulate others who are where you want to be. –Spiritually and socially. Apprentice yourself to them and become a student of life, not just academia. Escape and evade from those who you don't want to be like. Don't concern yourself with their opinion. Who cares? Fella's, focus like a laser on becoming a real man.

Finally, don't *ever* care what others think about you.[14] As mentioned earlier, be bullet-proof.

SAFE SPACES ARE A TREND that will hopefully fizzle out. However, without a concerted effort to discipline your verbal vomit on social platforms, it will be difficult to move on as a real man.

Safe space mentality is an issue that certainly needs addressed, but even worse is the narcissistic shift of the American culture. Everyday routine life has become the "reality show" on social platforms. When I muster the energy to look at social media to see how my family and friends are doing, I usually give up and close the app on my phone in exasperation; the effort to scroll through the pages of unless information is too tedious.

For example, we have to filter through advertisements, pictures of people eating at restaurants, adult's showing off new toys, and video bombardments of senseless acts created by others. Yet, worst of all, are the never-ending pictures of "ooh, ooh, look at me and my new picture of me!" –The absolute narcissistic vanity of social media users seems to have no limit.

**Real men don't need to take pictures of themselves in the mirror.**

As a rule of thumb, adhere to the following five rules when posting comments or pictures to social media:

1. Posting pictures of yourself should be limited, and have significant meaning. –Weddings, victories at sporting events, family reunions, vacations, proms and dances, new family pictures, etc. If at all possible, try to always include someone else in the photograph so you don't appear as a narcissist.

2. Limit re-posting; even if you think it's very important or funny. Odds are they already saw the post from someone else.

3. Never say anything negative on someone else's post. It's bad form. If you have an issue, say it privately.

4. Tolerate other people's views. For example, I know people that are Atheists. I am not an Atheist. Even though some of them try to goad me into argument, I refuse to participate. I remain neutral to their views; even though I believe they are wrong. I am willing to have a discussion if they are able to remain civil.

5. Don't send invites to people to participate in games. It's annoying. If they want to play Candy Crush, they will do

so without your guidance.

Higher education also suffers from social decay. No longer are students taught to think critically, but rather to conform to indoctrination standards antithetical to Christians. Your manliness is not dependent on the atheistic worldview. In fact, worldly education has little to do with learning wisdom or becoming a man. Benjamin Franklin and Abraham Lincoln were not strongly educated men by today's standard. Both were tempered, disciplined, had strong standing in their communities, and considered wise. Their manliness was shaped in tandem with their creator and the willingness to educate themselves. They did not require indoctrination.

Being a digital narcissist is unmanly. It proves that you are unsecure in your manhood. It proves that you need a checkup-from-the-neck-up. Be a real man and remember that you don't need to post pictures of yourself to get positive affirmation. Your self-worth comes from your quiet inner strength and your creator. Break free from the shackle of mental slavery and be a real man. You don't need a safe space to define who you are. Let go of the social media drug. It does not need to rule you. Don't incite conflict with others behind the screen of your device; instead, promote tolerance and civility.

PAT MCDONALD, AUTHOR of the paper *Narcissism in the Modern World*, said it perfectly: "Much of our distress comes from a sense of disconnection. We have a narcissistic society where self-promotion and individuality seem to be essential, yet in our hearts that's not what we want. We want to be part of a community, we want to be supported when we're struggling, and we want a sense of belonging. Being extraordinary is not a necessary component to being loved."[15]

**A real man loves his family and friends regardless of their attributes or faults.**

The ultimate goal for all real men is to leave a legacy. In the course of our life, we can accomplish this by pursuing two distinct paths: The path of love, or the path of hate.

Following the path of love, we strive to put the needs of others before our own. Consideration of others is always the course of our conversations and decisions. Following the path of love, we always try to be kind to others while being patient with those less inclined to do so. Don't let social media and digital narcissism dictate who you are. Be a real man and take control of both. Use social media as a communication tool and nothing else. –As it was meant to be. You will soon notice that your "real man" will emerge, and your need for a safe space will diminish.

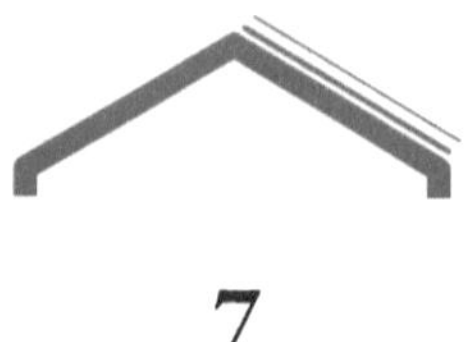

# 7

# Real Men Don't Allow Extended Family or Friends to Make Their Decisions

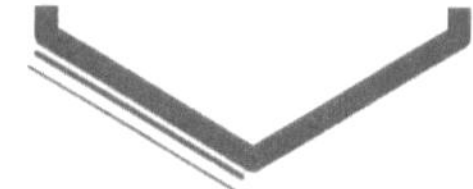

Every man has the *right* to be the Leader of his home and his family. This applies across the whole spectrum of influence in his life, but in this case, I just want to ask one question: Do you make decisions for yourself and your family, or does your Momma?

Ouch. That's a bitter pill.

Because our society is evolving into a "forever boy" culture, I am going to have difficulty making a case to some. "Why," you might ask? –Because, again, it's become the norm and therefore seen as an acceptable practice.

You can be eighteen to vote or die in war, but you cannot own a handgun or consume alcohol until the age of twenty-one.

I'll assume that if you are eighteen or older, you consider yourself a man. Have you concluded that you need to be taking care of yourself? Have you set a plan before yourself and started executing it? Are you ready to take the risk of being an adult and relieve your parents of the burden of caring for you? If not, why?

At age eighteen, I kissed my mother goodbye and joined the Army. However, I'd already begun thinking of a plan B if for some reason my enlistment didn't work out. In other words, I was already *mentally* aware of the fact that I was supposed to man-up and start taking care of myself. The Army just happened to be the route I wanted to take to do so.

Now, there is nothing wrong with a young man living at home while attending vocational training, college, or a university. This is a sensible plan. *But*, (and this is very important) it is his responsibility to take care of himself while respecting the home and rules of his parents. In other words, do your own laundry! You need to also manage your own finances and budget for your own expenses. (Though sneaking a home-cooked meal once in a while is highly recommended!)

TO BE A MAN YOU MUST know the difference between seeking advice, taking advice, and ignoring advice. When seeking advice, realize that you have to strongly consider the source. Taking advice from someone not qualified to give it is like seeking an appendectomy from a hair stylist. Why would you go there? You need to ask some very important questions before seeking or taking advice from anyone. For example, does the person you are seeking or taking advice from truly have your best interest in mind? Or, can you trust them? If you can't honestly answer *yes,* then you need not bother. Next, are you prepared to hear an answer you may not agree with? You may not like what advice you receive. Additionally, if more than one person you trust gives you advice counter to what you want to hear, consider what you're thinking of doing. You may be about to make a grave mistake.

Some time ago, I was considering taking a small business loan to start my own business. I carefully did the research and believed I could move forward with my plan. But, since I always seek the advice of those I trust prior to making big decisions that impact my family, I sought the counsel of several close friends. The first advice I got was in favor of my plan and I was encouraged. However, trusting my instincts, I sought the counsel of three additional friends. Two of which were somewhat older than me, so I wanted their perspective. I was dismayed to receive advice counter to what I wanted to hear from them both. In fact, they brought to light a very important issue that I was not considering seriously enough. Because of this I carefully selected a final person who I knew was very wise. I'd received counsel from this friend in the past and respected his opinion greatly. He also concurred with my two dissenting friends.

Having received this advice, I then carefully put additional thought into the business venture, did more research, then realized that my dissenting friends were correct. I was about to take too great a risk given the current status of my family. I concluded that a business venture was not a good idea for now, but could possibly pursue once my children were older and no longer in the home.

Receiving and taking quality advice does not imply you are not a man, in fact it is the opposite.

**Real men are willing to take advice before making life impacting decisions.**

Seeking and taking quality advice hasn't always been a priority for me. Because of this, I learned some very painful lessons in life. I've bought lemons that looked good on four wheels, but not so good under the hood, I've borrowed money when I wasn't in a position to pay it back, and I've lent money that I shouldn't have that cost me dearly financially.

Before I was married, I made decisions that sometimes resulted in severe consequences, though thankfully, never anything that involved incarceration.

As a young soldier in the Army, I remember waking up one weekend in the barracks thinking I needed an extended vacation. So, instead of seeking advice and doing it the right way by requesting leave, I turned my weekend pass into a three-day pass. Thinking back now, I have no idea what I thought was going to be the consequence of such a decision, but I did it anyway. Once I returned, I found myself standing in front of my Commander's desk at the position of attention.

"Specialist, if you needed time off, why didn't you ask your Platoon Sergeant or First Line Leader?" he asked with a puzzled look.

"I don't know, Sir," was all I could answer.

"You realize that I just can't have soldiers who are AWOL, right? What if everyone decided to not report for duty? Where do you think the Army would be and how would our readiness be effected?"

"I suppose I didn't think that one through, Sir," I mumbled with embarrassment.

"Well next time you want time off, you better ask for advice before you do something stupid again. Got it?"

"Yes, Sir."

"You're immediately reduced in rank by two grades and will serve forty-five days extra duty. –Dismissed."

The next forty-five days seemed to last a lifetime, and the loss of rank and pay didn't help matters either. However, I can say emphatically that I learned my lesson. I took my Commander's advice and was never late for duty again.

**Real men wisely take the advice of those who have experience.**

Though it is a great idea to seek the advice of those who have experience, it is just as prudent to ignore advice when you know it is unsound or negative. Unsound advice comes from those who have failed at what they are advising on, and negative advice comes from those who are "professional dream-killers."

I am married to an amazing woman who consents to me being the leader of our home. She blesses me with allowing me to make the big decisions, and oftentimes seeks my counsel on other issues as well. But most importantly, she trusts me to seek counsel with her before we decide on a course of action. It took us a few years, but this is what a marriage is supposed to look like.

Early in our marriage, we decided to have children, and today we have three amazing kids. However, there has never been a shortage of people who are willing to give advice on how to raise our children. Of course, there is nothing wrong with taking advice, but first, the advice has to filter through one important question: *Do I want my children to be like theirs?* If not, then politely ignore the advice.

The greatest offenders of giving advice when said advice is not asked for, are relatives. Can anyone relate here? Additionally, everyone believes that their way of raising kids is the best way. This is a great annoyance to me, though I believe others may feel the same.

I remember on one occasion when visiting a relative I corrected my daughter when addressing an adult. For example, my wife and

I teach our children to say "Miss Elizabeth" or "Mr. John" when addressing adults. The relative in question looked my daughter in the eye and said, "You don't have to say that to me, don't you listen to your daddy!" The relative's comments were said to be consoling, but I disagreed. Stepping in, I corrected that statement on the spot.

"We would prefer that she still address you as we have taught her," I stated as politely as I could. "These are our rules."

"Well," the relative said a little indignantly, "that is a silly rule and you should not make her do that."

I chose to ignore the advice of my relative. I did not seek the advice so therefore it shouldn't have been given. —And in the end, the relative was being disrespectful to our family rules. However, I politely let the issue go to avoid further conflict. Additionally, I did pull my daughter aside and explain to her why it was respectful to address adults the way she was being taught. Ironically, as children typically are, she was oblivious to the whole tone of the conversation and left with an "Ok, Daddy" and a skip in her step.

This may seem trivial, but often more than not, children remember the teachable moments more so than the whole lesson. **Real men ignore advice that is counter to their goals or toxic in nature.**

THE MOST POWERFUL ASSET a man can have is his family. Your mother, father, brother, or sister love you (hopefully) and believe that they have your best interests in mind. However, sometimes their best intentions can be a dream-killer.

As I briefly stated in the first chapter, I managed to graduate high school with no plan for the future. I congratulated myself on how "smart" I was fooling the system by doing as little as possible and still receiving a diploma. I was quite impressed with myself.

Then reality set in.

Six months later I was still flipping burgers at a restaurant listening to my friends talk about the classes they were enrolled in and how much fun they were having in college. While they were excited and dreaming about the future, I was not excited about being promoted to Head Cook.

Have you ever had one of those moments in life when everything becomes absolutely clear? When you realize that, right now at this very moment, everything is about to change? That no matter what you won't be stopped? I had one of those moments standing over a charbroil grill watching a steak sizzle. In that steak, I could see the next twenty years of my life. I remember looking to my right at the other end of the kitchen. There stood another cook doing what I was doing. He also was preparing food. However, he was in his mid-thirties. –A grandpa to a teenager. In him, I could see me. I saw my future. It wasn't a future I wanted. I wanted to alter my ship's course.

I knew something had changed. No matter what, I was going to do something. –And before my shift ended that day, I knew I was going to join the Army and see the world.

To give a little back history, I'm blind in my left eye. I lost vision due to an accident with a pair of scissors when I was eight years old. So, when I announced to friends and family I was going to join the Army, my dream was squashed immediately.

"The Army doesn't take people who are half blind," some advised. "Don't bother trying." These dream-killers just about rocked me out of my future. But something pushed me to try anyway.

## Real men trust their instincts and flush negative influence from relatives and friends.

Ever since I was little, I had a budding dream to fly. Truthfully, I really wanted to be an Astronaut. –No, seriously, I *really* wanted to be one. But, once I lost my vision, I knew this wasn't going to happen. Somewhere in my youth, I'd learned that being in the Air Force could lead to a flying career in NASA. So, I started there clinging to a shred of a dream.

I left the Air Force recruiter office twenty minutes later pretty miffed. They were not interested in a half-blind Airman.

I then tried the Navy. I got the same result there.

I then stood looking at two doors that were side by side. One said Marines, the other Army. I knew pretty much that the Marines meant I was going to get killed in training, so I went into the Army office.

Waiting to be called to a recruiter desk, I was almost resigned to hear the same answer.[16]

"Mr. Durst?"

I looked up to see a recruiter who appeared to be carved out of steel, and then rolled in a brand-new uniform made of complete starch. The man had more ribbons than a parade of Brownie Scouts.

"Yeah, that's me," I answered.

"Come on back to my desk and let's go over your pre-qualification questions."

I followed mournfully knowing where this was going to go.

"Says here, you're blind in your left eye," he said looking over the top of his glasses.

"What makes you think you can be in the Army with one eye working?"

"Offended at his question, I puffed up and replied, "I can already shoot fine with one eye, and I can run. How complicated can it be?" I countered back.

Leaning back in his chair and studying me for several minutes, he finally replied, "I'll give it a shot. The Army has relaxed some of their requirements lately, and you might be able to get in."

"Alright!" I exclaimed with excitement. "When can I enlist?"

"Hold your horses," he said holding up his hand. "This is going to be a lengthy process. We have to get you medically approved. It may take months. Are you prepared to go the distance? Or, will I be wasting my time?"

I smiled slightly and knew I'd finally cracked the door.

"You say where to be, I'll be there," I promised. "Let's do it."

I had made my decision, and I didn't need my mother to approve it.

FOR THE NEXT TWO AND a half years I served as an Infantryman in Germany. Once my tour was over, I returned home rather than re-enlist. The memory of that day sweating over a burger grill still burned in my mind. *What was next?*

I started to think that I might, just might, be able to go to college. It seemed an impossible dream, yet I clung to it. This was briefly stated in the first chapter.

Now, attending college in the nineties was still more of a rarity in my home state of West Virginia than it is today. In addition, no one in my immediate family, besides an uncle, had *ever* attended college. My family was a blue-collar family and always had been.[17] –And so, it began....

"No one has ever gone to college in our family." Or, "you barely graduated high school!" Chuckle, chuckle, snort snort…. "You just don't have the grades!"

**Real men don't allow their family or friends to make their decisions for them.**

Exactly four years later in 1997, I hung my college degree on the wall, then stepped back to take a good look.

I still remember folding my arms and smiling with great satisfaction.

DON'T ALLOW YOUR EXTENDED family, friends, or parents to make your decisions. Be a real man.

Seeking advice is always a good idea, but be sure you weigh the difference of whether or not your getting constructive criticism, or just wasting time with a dream-killer. Don't wander aimlessly waiting for someone else to decide for you. Weigh your options, seek advice, flush negativity, then man up and make your decision.

If the decision turns ill, then you'll at least have the satisfaction that your standing on the ashes of your own merit and the decision *you* made. –And the experience will be much more valuable to you than if it was made by someone else.

# 8

# Real Men Treat Women with Respect

"Husbands, love your wives, and do not be harsh with them."
Colossians 3:19, ESV

There is no greater loser than a man who treats women as property or objects. Our culture and society are consumed with the idea of dominating women sexually, socially, and parading them as trophies in some make-believe conquest. Shamefully, this destroys families and marriages. It's disgraceful.

**Real men cherish, protect, and respect women.**

Some time ago, football player Ray Rice made international news by battering his girlfriend in an elevator. A hard hook rendered her unconscious. The video then played around the world once it was made public.

How does a man get to a place where he feels comfortable battering a woman? Sadly, this type of behavior may be spotlighted in the world of sports, but it's also pervasive in our society as a whole.

In America, about 41% of women experienced contact sexual violence, physical violence, and/or stalking by an intimate partner and reported an intimate partner violence-related impact during their lifetime.[18] That is astounding. What is wrong, men? Why are we doing these things to our wives, fiancés, or girlfriends? How have we allowed ourselves to be so weak-minded or so socially unfit we need to lash out physically harming those we care about?

Part of the problem is the cycle of perpetuity. Children are often witness to domestic violence. This is observed by young boys who believe this is how to conduct themselves once they become men.

The happy end to Ray Rice's story is worth noting, however. Though he committed a horrible act that cost him his career, he owned up to it like a man. His battering of his now wife, Janay, will be something he will always have to live with. But after the incident, he sought and received help. Now, he is a strong advocate against domestic abuse, and continues to work towards supporting those efforts today. Well done, Ray.

**A real man will always seek to put the needs of women before his own.**

IF YOU QUOTE THE ABOVE statement to a modern liberal thinker, they will likely be repulsed by the idea. Ignore the protests.

As early as 1848, the women's rights movement, also known as women's suffrage, petitioned our society for equal constitutional privileges. The cause was just and warranted. By 1920, the $19^{th}$ Amendment changed the electoral status of our country forever. Nonetheless, the modern liberal cause has warped this victory into a dysfunctional social relation between the sexes. It is no longer agreeable for a man to open a car or building door for a woman in some places. It is no longer agreeable for a man to seek the leadership of his family or even to be the protector of the home.

Women who are single parents are championed as the social winners of a decaying family fabric that is producing gender-confused children that have no basic discipline skills. –And yes, there are exceptions to every rule, but overall, this is indisputable.

To compound the issue, men in our society have been more than willing to allow this to happen. Somewhat lazy by nature, many men willingly step aside when given the option. Others ignore the responsibility of being present to raise or manage a family. This has to be corrected. It is up to us to right the ship and hold the rudder on course. –Not by returning to old habits by dominating women, but by insisting on equal partnerships in marriage and by taking leadership. Leadership does not equal conqueror. Leadership means being willing to make decisions for the betterment of the family, even if those decisions are extremely difficult to make. Leadership also means putting your interests and wants *last*, and those of your families *first*. –And that includes your time.

Most American men work long hours. It's what we do. If we work a typical job with typical hours, we usually rise about the time it's getting light outside, and get home when it starts to get dark. It's not uncommon to work more than a normal eight-hour shift. So, by the time we get home, we just want to shut down.

Have you ever heard the questions, "Honey, can you help the kids with some of their homework or reading?" Or, "Can you look at the toilet? It's not flushing again."

These are everyday issues or problems that we all, as men, have to deal with. How do you react? Do you grumble or complain? Is there a game coming on that is more important? Or, do you handle the problems that you are asked to solve?

Some time back, my wife and I made the decision to cancel our satellite television programming. Truth be told, we rarely used it anyway, but to seal the deal to maximize our time, we eliminated it. We still watch the occasional DVD or something on Netflix, but it's with the understanding that work comes before play. Our children grumbled at first. Nonetheless, we read to them, helped with any school work, completed chores, etc. And, more importantly, it's not all done by my wife. I take leadership responsibility of my family and do these things with or without her help; because there are days she just needs a break.

Sometimes, no, oftentimes, a woman's needs are not asked, but blaringly evident. Women are not the problem in most cases. It's the men who can't seem to remember that they are equal to us, not subservient. It's nice when my wife has dinner waiting on the stove when I get home, but she knows I'd never demand it. As homeschooler's, she has always worked through the day educating our children; and somehow, the house magically stays clean and the laundry stays caught up. She even runs a business part-time. Again, not because I make any demands, but because that is the partnership we pursue. If she could make more money outside the home than I could, she might decide to do so. It'd be her decision. –And pursuant of an equal partnership, I'd do whatever would be necessary to help manage our household.

In early 2010, I returned from the Iraq War. The experience was not pleasant, and given the environment, it was easy to forget the consideration needed for a peaceful marriage. My wife, Barbara, and I still loved each other very much, but something was different. Since I had been gone for over a year, she had to step up to the plate and be the 'man of the house' as well as the mother. Over time, she grew efficient in doing things her way. Successfully, she managed our finances, raised and disciplined our children, handled the affairs of our household, directed all the maintenance of our home and vehicles, ensured the children attended school, and juggled countless other things I can't even imagine. She even weathered the home and children through a tornado while I was half-a-world away. So, when I returned home from the war, she had difficulty returning management of some of these things to me.

In return, I proceeded to explain to her everything she was doing wrong while I was away, and pushed her too hard and too fast to go back to the way things were before.

Our contention nearly brought us to divorce; and though both of us were failing to compromise, God helped us to find discernment.

Putting her issues aside and looking at mine, I failed to respect her as an equal partner in our marriage. This was also a large part of her unhappiness during the whole ordeal.

As men it is difficult to tamper our pride and temper our anger. It's the way we are wired. God created us to be warriors & protectors. We need to be aware of this and work hard not to apply these strengths against our families. We're to use them to protect the ones we love, not to do them harm.

**A Real man will always seek ways to demonstrate his respect to a woman.**

Many years ago, in our marriage, my wife and I lived poorly in a one-bedroom apartment on the wrong side of town. However, the rent was cheap, and because I was finishing an undergraduate degree, we elected to ignore the consistent drug raids around us. It was a common occurrence to hear pounding on neighboring doors and the words, "open up, police!"

We also invested in an additional lock for the door.

On one ordinary evening, Barbara had lovingly taken the time to make us a spaghetti dinner. Once ready, she called me to eat. Working on some coursework, that now seems insignificant, but at the time apparently *was* important; I called out, "Ok. Give me a couple more minutes."

She called out again. "The food's getting cold! Come eat!"

"Almost done," I insisted.

Clearly, I took longer than I had realized, because suddenly I heard the loud clatter of a plate hitting the floor.

Rising and going to our small kitchenette, I saw spaghetti sliding down the wall just above the trashcan.

"Is there something wrong?!" I asked angrily.

"Nothing," she replied calmly. "Just cleaning up the dishes."

While some of you may be laughing right now, let me just add that both of us were so stubborn over that fight that the spaghetti not only dried and stayed on the wall for over a week, it would have remained if her mother hadn't cleaned it up for the both of us.

No man is perfect, but over the years, I have learned to be more attentive and praiseful to my wife. Not because I want to be some sniveling suck-up to gain her favor, or because she is an overbearing woman that demands it; but because she genuinely deserves it.

Women truly are the grease that keeps the wheel of the world moving. As men, we would do well to remember it more often.

**A real man will respect the wisdom of women.**

HOLIDAYS, BIRTHDAYS, special occasions, and anniversaries are allusive moments in a man's life. There have been days when I have literally showed up to participate. Personally, my struggle has always been Holiday's. At times, I get so focused on the routine of work and home maintenance, that I lose sight of the special moments.

Amazingly, my wife never forgets or misses a beat. She juggles a much busier schedule than I do, but still finds time for those special moments. She plans, organizes, and procures all the necessary things for each and every birthday, holiday, or special moment. In addition, she oftentimes does the same for members of our church and community. Because of this, I respect her requests to be there when I am supposed to be.

Men, nothing makes a woman more bitter than for her husband to makes excuses for not attending important events. They may not be important to us, (and full disclosure, sometimes they don't feel too important to me either) but special events are very important to them. Honor your wife and family and be there when it counts. Don't allow work to interfere. Stand your ground with your employer. If you can take the time off, do so.

Exceptions being the rule, there are times you will miss events. Because of the Army, I have missed many. However, I've learned to cherish the moments I do get because of this. Don't purposefully dodge your family. Not only does it stress your marriage, it emotionally harms your children.

Growing up, I remember many birthdays forgotten by my father. The feeling was not pleasant. It obviously had a lasting impact on me since I remember to this day. Don't be the father that does not commit time to his family. Nothing is more damaging.

If you are like me, you will remain blissfully unaware of all the nuances required to celebrate holidays, birthdays, and special occasions. The important part is just showing up. As a man and a father, that's more than enough!

## Real men enter the partnership of marriage before having children.

A MAN THAT I KNOW PERSONALLY experienced the following, and insisted that I share his story:

*The greatest sin I ever committed was the murder of my own child. I've prayed for, and received, forgiveness for my actions; but I know that someday I will meet my child face-to-face. It is then that I will seek closure.*

*Very few days go by that I'm not haunted by the shameful decision I made the summer of 1993 to abort my first child. I was not a Christian man at the time, but recently having left the Army, I was preparing to start my college education. It was then that I met and began a relationship with a young lady. After some time, she got pregnant.*

*I remember thinking at the time that I didn't have time for such an inconvenience. In my selfishness, I only thought of myself and my future goals. I didn't have time to deal with an unexpected child in my life.*

*The young lady I was involved with was not in support of having an abortion, but allowed me to persuade her to my way of thinking.*

*Right at that moment, I should have respected her belief that it was wrong. —I should have manned-up and done the right thing. However, all I could think of was my own selfish needs. My lack of faith and moral understanding allowed me to commit the intolerable act of murder.*

*To this day, I'm still ashamed.*

As men, we are not gods. We have been blessed by our creator in superior strength to women, larger stature, and a more attuned willingness to fight. But these gifts were granted to be the protectors of our families, not the destroyer of them.

IN CHRISTIAN MARRIAGES, only Lutheran's specifically have the word *help* in their marriage vows. It is strange that all vows don't include the word *help*. It is the most important ingredient in marriage. It's a partnership of equal labor. –This includes children.

I remember when my son, Ryan, came into the world. He has Down Syndrome and Autism. Initially, there was shock, and then determination. –Determination that, no matter what, I'd love my child and do my best to raise him.

Today, it's been over twenty years, and my wife still shoulders the burden of caring for him while caring for our two younger children. In fact, we both patiently manage his needs, which are many, even though he is a fully grown adult. Even simple chores like bathing requires our assistance. Yet again, this usually falls under her supervision if I am working or not home. It amazes me how much nurturing capacity she has and how she can keep up with it all.

However, the point being made is, even with the great skills women have, it is not their sole responsibility to care for the children while men pursue relaxing activities every weekend because of a *hard week at work.* These things are occasionally okay, but with the understanding that sometimes there needs to be a 'Mom's day out' as well.

ONCE CHILDREN ARE BORN, they become the centerpiece of the marriage. Everything else becomes second except your relationship with each other and God the Father before that. We're not to spoil our children –Life's lessons are always important– but we care for them and allow them to grow and learn. We allow some mistakes so that experience can develop into wisdom, but protect them from other mistakes to prevent serious harm. This shapes and molds them into healthy members of society once our parenting needs are completed.

Children are the perfect gift from God. They are born free from an adult's failures or problems, and utterly reliant upon us. Therefore, be a man and commit to a healthy marriage before you take on the responsibility of caring for God's perfect creation. Children are the supreme responsibility gifted to us, and the source of our immortality. No amount of wealth, power, entertainment, or fame will last forever. –These things are simply the byproducts of life and fleeting in the moment. But the children you rear will perpetuate parts of you till the end of time. –For good or ill.

9

# Real Men Raise Their Own Kids Instead of Letting Someone, or Something Else, Do So

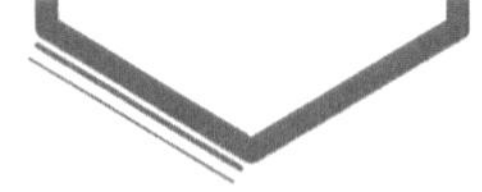

"Whoever spares the rod hates his son, but he who loves him is diligent to discipline him."
Proverbs 13:24, ESV

A real man takes responsibility for raising his own kids. This is the single most pressing issue of our time. Today, men have accepted the role of subordinate, or even absentee, when children are concerned. Children have simply become the byproduct of promiscuity that are simply shrugged off and tolerated at best. Because there is only sexual conquest involved, family structure and unity are not even part of the equation. Children, then, are simply marginalized, and usually ignored by their father's. In some cases, the children are not even acknowledged as existing.

A real man does none of these things. A real man will abstain from having children until they can be properly protected and nurtured as a family through marriage. A real man will protect his offspring at all cost from the evil of the world until the time is right to carefully expose them to all that they must endure as a young adult. A real man will do everything in his power to protect the

75

sanctimony of his marriage; thereby protecting his children from the social decay of modern society. A real man will do all these things for his children and family.

**A real man will fight to the death to protect his family so that his children may prosper and learn by his example.**

Two things will kill the love of a child's heart for their father: No time, and no praise.

To be blunt, as a man, you immediately yield the right to what *you* need, and are required to give your family what *they* need. You become the last one on the totem pole. You address your children's needs first, then your wife's, and finally, if you have the time and resources remaining, you address your own. Part of addressing your children's needs first is giving them time.

A real man will not just provide for his family, he will commit time to it. It is often very difficult to work a fifty-hour week, especially if a laborer, and then muster the energy to spend time with your children. However, this must be done. In fact, it is critical to the development of your children. A real man does not flop on the couch the whole weekend and watch football. A real man will spend time with his wife and children first. A real man does not run away every weekend to "go fishing" or pursue other recreation while leaving his children at home wondering who their father is. And a real man does not pawn off his kids to friends and relatives so that he can selfishly pursue his own interests. There is nothing wrong with taking personal time, but these moments should be the exception and not the rule; and never at the expense of the family.

A very good friend of mine is married, and part of that marriage involves a stepdaughter from his wife's first marriage. To his credit, he does an amazing job with the stepdaughter treating her as his own.

From time to time, he and his wife, as part of the court settlement, must take the stepdaughter to see her father. The father lives out of state, so travel involves some time.

As told to me by my friend, the same scenario plays out in this young girl's life each weekend she visits.

Once she meets her father, he immediately takes her to his parents (her grandparents) house. Once there, he hugs her and bids her adieu. The young girl spends the entire time with her grandparents instead of with her father. Once the weekend is over, he picks her back up and takes her back to meet my friend and his wife.

Because I have been military most of my life, my first instinct is that I want to punch this guy in his face, but then I remember that my Pastor wants me to be a better man and I realize prayer would be a better route.

My heart aches for this young girl who simply wants to be with her father. Yet, he is still mentally living the life of a boy, and refuses to grow up and take responsibility for his daughter.

A real man would lovingly take his daughter and cherish every moment he had with her regardless of the divorce. He would do everything in his power to be part of her life regardless of the distance involved.

Because children almost *always* blame themselves for their parents' divorce, tremendous effort must be made to counter this by dedicating time to them.

**A real man will give time to his children at every opportunity.**

From a personal perspective, I can say I was very lucky, but more than likely just very blessed. My own mother divorced early and then remarried a few years later. With three children in tow, she entered another marriage to a man that, by any reasonable measurement, did an amazing job. Was he perfect? –Of course not. Were mistakes made? –Sure. Were there ever arguments? –You bet. –Lots of those! But one very critical thing he did do well was man up and *be a dad!*

If I recall correctly, I was six or seven when my step-father, Tom, married my mother. Though two more children eventually blessed the home, he performed his duties as a father with no prejudice. Only as an adult can I fully appreciate his sacrifice.

Food, clothing, health care, and a wholesome environment eased the anxiety in my life. Being as young as I was, most would argue that I had no conception of what life I was living. I'd argue otherwise. I fully remember, prior to my mother getting re-married, the struggles she endured. –The winter nights with marginal heat. She would warm our beds with a hairdryer because our rooms were so cold. When coal could not be afforded, (the apartment furnace was still heated with a coal fired boiler) she would take an old battered electric heater and place it in the hallway between me and my twin brethren's room, and my older sister's room. I also remember how we would crawl from our beds dragging a pillow and blanket from our beds to lay in front of the heater falling fast asleep; only to wake the next morning back in our beds. I also remember mom's bed was just a box frame on cinder blocks.

I remember nights on end being at a babysitter's house, lined up on the floor with a blanket, barely keeping my eyes open, waiting for our mother to pick us up after a long night working as a waitress trying to makes ends meet. I remember all these things. I remember being anxious. I remember sensing that something was terribly wrong. I remember seeing the worry and strain in my mother's face day after day. –Not knowing that she was constantly fighting to keep bills paid and food available, but knowing something was wrong nonetheless. I remember it all.

So, when these things are removed from a child's life, as what happened when she remarried, life assumes a routine and comfort important for a child to feel safe and nurtured. This is what Tom provided.

He did not try to pawn his three stepchildren off to another relative on our mother's side. He was a man and took in three children with open arms. He manned up and provided wholesome food for us to eat at the expense of his labor. –Sweating for years in a hot commercial bakery. He was a real man and dedicated time to us when not working; taking us on weekend trips and annual vacations. He didn't dash off and leave us for "relief" from work or the stress of the world. He was a real man.

Tom didn't sit in front of the TV every day. He spent time with us and made time at the dinner table a central part of our lives. –A lesson I still apply to my own family today.

Tom was man enough to take my twin brother and me by the hand and teach us some outdoor skills. –Fishing, hiking, and hunting. He encouraged us to join the Boy Scouts and apply ourselves to this adventure. Through him, my brother and I learned to appreciate the intoxicating freedom of nature and all that God has provided us. Tom did what a real man was supposed to do. He did not ignore us. He was our *Dad.*

And where was our father? He was absent. Though I love my father, and he has expressed much regret not spending more time with us, he was largely absent. He missed years of time and memories that he could have built. He did not perform as a real man and take responsibility for his children. There is no malice to this statement, just an expression of the facts. My father was more comfortable pursuing his own interests. –Because his father did the same, he followed this philosophy with his own children.

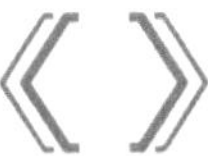

CHILDREN CAN OVERCOME just about anything. They are the most resilient of all God's creation. Yet, one thing that is the hardest for them to survive is neglect.

What is the difference between healthy well-adjusted children and those that appear to be social failures? Largely its due to failing and unstable families. I'd wager this is the cause of the rise of homosexuality in males as young boys struggle to identify with their sex in the absence of a father.

In addition to this, some parents use technology as a nanny for raising their children. –And without the nurturing input of parents and community, basic relational skills, and even self-confidence, are usually missing as children mature.

Technology is a wonderful thing, *if* used in moderation. Like sugary drinks, too much can kill you. This is the view a real man must have in regards to technology as it relates to the development of his children.

When a child is allowed to spend day after day at a game console or a computer, it is equivalent to poisoning their food with arsenic. Or similarly, it is like the smoker's dilemma when smoking one cigarette at a time: You will die of cancer. It's just a matter of when.

An entire book could be dedicated to the issue of technology in the lives of children; however, I would like to emphasize, that I believe entertainment addiction and instant gratification are the two most significant issues facing our society as we struggle to learn how to adapt to the overwhelming advances to modern technologies.[19]

As it relates to being a man, you simply cannot use media as a babysitting tool. This quickly warps into the sole source of their intellectual and social instruction, and the end result is already becoming evident in the today's youth.

**A real man does not parent through a game console, nor does he allow technology to raise his children.**

Children are the most precious resource we have. Real men simply cannot waiver on the issue of quality rearing. Nothing else should have a higher priority, and our children should always be paramount to our daily purpose.

Be a real man. Take charge of all the things that threaten to take over the rearing of your children. Do whatever it takes to protect them. –Whatever it takes! Intercede each and every time someone threatens the harmony in your home. Fiercely protect your children's development. Once you establish your boundaries, let no one compromise them.

Rid yourself of technology overload. Keep media from sucking the life out of your family. Closely monitor technology and only allow it to serve its purpose, don't let it rule you or your family. Only you have the power to control it. Only you bear the responsibility if you don't.

In short, be a man.

DISCIPLINING YOUR CHILDREN is tough. As men, we must be clear with our spouses as to how to discipline. Be sure that you have a good understanding on the expectation before you have children. I can promise you they will require it.

My wife and I are believers of corporal punishment. However, what we consider corporal is not what most have in mind. First, mother was the primary discipliner. She was willing to take the lead, and since she was the parent who was with our children the most, it made sense that she would be respected this way by the children. When required, she would be perfectly comfortable using her wooden spoon. This usually involved a couple swats, but in the eyes of our children, it proved that a line of demarcation had been reached. This was the no-crossing point of their undesired behavior.

To be clear, if my wife was giving a swat or two, then our kids had already exhausted their warnings and time-outs. In fact, if they persisted, then things would elevate to stage two. Stage two was dad getting involved; and if that happened, then the kids knew they were in big trouble. This was by design. It gave their mother a way out and a tool that, if she had to use it, the kids knew it was bad.

## Real men are willing to discipline their children when required.

If a father needs to discipline a child, then it is important that it is done the right way. First, I never would whip my children while angry. This is dangerous. As men, our strength and size can seriously hurt or injure a child. Don't do it. Take time to cool off. Use the time to have your disobedient child explain to you why they are getting a whipping. Ask questions like, "how many smacks do you think you deserve? Where do you want your whipping? What did you do that you deserve the whipping you are about to get?" Honestly by the time I spent 10-15 minutes asking these questions and cooling off, I could barely swing the belt. Even then, when I barely tapped my kids' little butts, they were more upset over the fact they had to get a whipping and crying their eyeballs out. I could barely do it after that. But, the lesson was learned: I did something that crossed the line. I need to work hard on not doing that again.

Children need to know what lines they cannot cross. Parents that do not hold that line have unruly children and constantly have to deal with disrespect. Do not spare the rod even if you use it sparingly and lightly. If you do, you will struggle keeping your children under control.

Proper discipline teaches your children to have respect and to be obedient when they are older. It helps them to learn to mature beyond their selfish desires and to be respectful to others. It's hard work, but so worth it in the end.

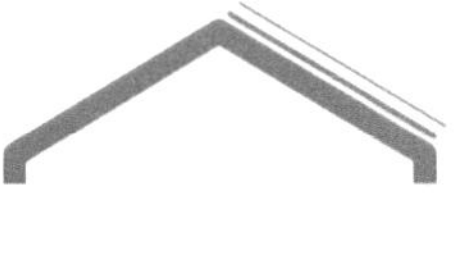

# 10

# Real Men Teach Their Children

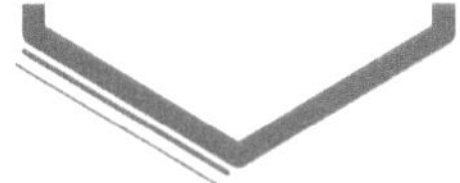

"I will instruct you and teach you in the way you should go; I will counsel you with my eye upon you."
Psalm 32:8, ESV

Being young and single is fun. It allows you to flex your new-found independence and to focus on what you want to pursue in life. However, even if you are single or newly married, I believe it's worth your time to read through this chapter. The day may come when you will have children, and deciding the best way to teach them will be important.

Children are the real test of a man's legacy. Will your children have a life of failure? Or, will your children grow into responsible adults that take your example and mentorship forward to your grandchildren? The answer is: Both.

There is absolutely nothing you can do to prevent an adult from choosing to fail; other than do your absolute best to pass on wisdom while they are young. Because we all have the choice of free will once we are adults, we decide as individuals the road we want to walk on. This same choice is also freely given by our Father God, so why would we assume, as Father's ourselves, we could control it any differently?

The only thing we can control is our own example and what we choose to teach our children. From here, we can only pray they apply what they have learned.

I believe, outside of the Word of God, we should also teach our children:

1. Life survival skills
2. A strong work ethic
3. Money management
4. Respect for other's and different opinions
5. To stand firm in their beliefs
6. To earn luxuries
7. To contribute to the family
8. How to be a life-long learner

Did you say life survival skills? Yep. I sure did. I refer you to my comments in the first chapter about the Great Depression and the Dust Bowl. The food stopped coming to the local city grocer's, or because of unemployment, available food was unattainable. –And if it happened once, it will happen again. So why not have basic skills to at least be able to feed yourself?

No one needs to be a deerskin-wearing hunter that breaks trees with their bare hands and uses tree limbs for toothpicks, but for goodness sake, a real man should be able to competently hunt, fish, forage, and navigate in the wild. Also, a real man should know basic gardening skills for growing simple crops, and how to store for winter use. Simply stated, are you teaching these skills to your children?

I remember on one hunting occasion I was blessed with a large buck that had an equally large rack. I field dressed it and brought it home.

Once I pulled into the driveway, my youngest son and daughter jumped in the back of the truck and was amazed as to how big the deer was. I'd been hunting before, and enjoy the experience each year, but this time they were old enough to really remember it and were excited.

"That's a big deer, Dad," Emily stated with bulging eyes. "Are you going to keep it?"

Laughing at her question, I replied, "You bet. I'm going to let it hang overnight and process the deer tomorrow."

"What's that mean?" little Ethan asked.

"Well, I'm going to skin the deer then butcher the meat."

"Wow!" Emily exclaimed. "Can we watch?"

"I'll do better than that. I'll let you help!"

They both whooped in excitement.

The following day, as I had promised, we skinned the deer and then butchered the meat. I specifically remember weighing out seventy-two pounds of meat. –A pretty good size deer by any standard.

What is important is that, instead of pushing my children aside, I used the experience to teach both my daughter and son the value and purpose of hunting for meat. They both helped skin that deer and also to butcher it. By allowing them to get their own hands in the process, I was able to teach them a useful skill. I'm sure they will want to help again the next time I go hunting, and no matter if they ever choose to hunt themselves as adults, they will at least know the skill if ever needed.

It's the same with every outdoor skill. When fishing, I don't fish, they do. This enables me to focus on helping them master the skill.

In the back yard, I have a bb-gun target and a bow-and-arrow target. Whenever the kids want, they grab their guns or bows and do a little target practice.

They love it.

A SHORT TIME AGO, WE spent a Saturday in a state park. We spent most of the day hiking while my wife and I "guarded the rear." Emily and Ethan were our "scouts" to ensure that we didn't lose the trail. Of course, my wife and I knew the trail was well marked, but as young children, they felt brave and confident by running far ahead to ensure we didn't get lost. They were quite specific in letting us know that each time we saw an orange diamond, we were on the trail. –And to not deviate from their approved route.

As they get older, I plan to take their navigational skills further by teaching them the specific value of a topographic map. –How to read the terrain, how determine locations by using a point of reference and a compass, and many other things. They will also know how to build fires and how to construct shelters. And when they are ready, I will take them hiking cross-country so that they can apply the skills they have learned.

**Real men use their child's natural curiosity as an instructional tool for teachable moments.**

LIFE IS TOUGH. BUT the moments we all cherish are those that create memories. Memories are the only insurance we have that makes our family permanent. For this reason, we need to make as many memories as possible. However, if it's done at the expense of hard work and self-discipline, then there is no value to the memories.

One of the most important lessons we can teach our children is the value of hard work. It hones self-discipline at an early age by showing that reward comes from effort. –Not the other way around.

In our home, our children are expected to work. When the home needs cleaned, they are expected to work. When rooms need tidied up, they are expected to work. If our children fail to perform the work, and don't do it in a quality manner, then the rewards go away. It's a recipe that sounds so simple, yet some fail to grasp the concept. This refers back to being an involved parent, not a friend to your children.

**Real men realize that to truly love their children, they cannot be their friend.**

MANY YEARS AGO AS A teenager, I failed to grasp the concept that my mother was not my friend. She chose, instead, to be a parent. Day after day I would hound my mother to drive the family car. After all that griping, she only let me use it once: To take my driver's test. Once I passed the test, she bluntly said, "Now buy your own car."

At age fifteen, I got a worker permit and took my first job working in a sandwich deli. I've been working ever since. I worked hard. Hours put in after school and on weekends, I finally saved up money for a car. I answered a want ad for a 1967 Buick Skylark. It was being sold by an elderly woman that was cleaning out her garage. I put five hundred cash in her hand (I know, that doesn't sound like a lot today, but it was then) and took my new wheels home. Soon I had it in my father's garage. He helped me put in a new water pump, clean out the distributor cap, put on new brakes, a new radiator with hoses, and add fresh oil. With some new tires, everything else on the car was still in working order.

Pea green and ugly, I drove that car proudly until I joined the Army. Why? Because I earned it. I worked hard for it. I worked hard to get it running, and it was mine. In other words, with hard work came the reward.

My mother was a wise parent. She knew full well I would appreciate a car I had worked for, and not one given to me.[20]

This is the lesson a real man will pass to his children. –That hard work always yields reward. Real men are not afraid to work and set an example to their children. Real men allow their children to work with them so that their children can learn from their example.

Be a man and get to work.

SOMETIMES, HOWEVER, it's very easy to get lost in work and ignore other problems. –Problems that can destroy.

Question: What is the number one problem with adults and marriage in general? –Money. –Or the mismanagement thereof.

I can honestly say that, as a young adult, I kept a pretty cool head about finances, but nonetheless, I still made some mistakes that got me in hot water. Nonetheless, I took responsibility for those mistakes and corrected them. One of my mistakes took *years* to overcome.[21]

**Real men don't whine to their parents for money.**

Managing money had to be a self-taught skill for me, however, real men don't throw their children to the wolves, they teach and instruct on how to manage money. To do this, parents have to resist the taboo of keeping their finances secretive from their children. They certainly don't need the passwords to your bank accounts, but they definitely need to see you manage your money.

Early money management skills should be a part of raising children. To start, give an allowance for work performed around the home; coupled with saving a portion of the money in a bank account. –And your children should be making the deposits, not you. But as your children get older, they need to see money *work* in their lives. The only way they can get a full picture of this, is to sit beside you as you distribute your money (pay bills) each month. –And the only way to do this is to have a budget.

**Real men don't use their money to pay bills then spend the rest. Every penny is accounted for.**

Be a real man and know where your money is going. This will be discussed further in the next chapter, so teach this knowledge to your children. Open your budget, work through it while your children watch. Let them see you dedicate every penny you earn to its appropriate place. Do this repeatedly so that they see you are serious and disciplined in your methods. Be a man and don't let your pride get in the way. Don't be concerned with whether or not your children know how much money you make each month. Real men aren't defined by their job, business, or income.

WELL MANAGED FINANCES develop a real man's self-confidence. However, having a strong self-image or personality does not permit you to be rude to others. –*Especially* when you realize that someone you are having a conversation with has a starkly different opinion than you do.

There is an old adage that says, "Never argue with a fool, for others watching cannot tell the difference." This has always been an important marker that I mentally reference whenever I find myself about to enter into a heated discussion. We all have been there and will continue to have encounters like this for the rest of our lives. Nonetheless, a real man will teach his children the art of self-intervention when guiding a conversation to rationality and calm. Observe the following rules:

- Respect other's opinions whether you agree or not.

There are times when you simply don't need to expend the effort to sway others to your opinion. Learn to recognize this early in a conversation. Teach this skill to your children. Not only will you save a great deal of time, but:

**A real man doesn't feel the need to force his opinion on others to validate his own self-image.**

- Never be rude or uncivil.

Too often in modern society the belief is held that, if you don't have the same opinion of someone that disagrees with you, that somehow makes you wrong. It is fortunate that this wasn't the case at the founding of our nation, if so, it's highly probable our constitution would have never been written or even ratified.

It's human to disagree; but a real man can agree to disagree. There is nothing wrong with a hardy argument kept within the confines of civility and even tones, but when neither participant can sway the argument, shake hands and change the subject. Be a real man and respect the opinions of others without losing your civility. Children need to observe this skill early in their development. Unfortunately, they will always do what you do and not so much what you say. Therefore, model this behavior and your children will learn from your example.

- Never lose you cool.

George Washington was a master conversationalist. The amount of study and thought he applied to the simple skill of conversation and company puts us all to shame in the modern era.[22] From his example we learn that: "When you deliver a matter do it without passion & with discretion, however mean the person be you do it too."

- Don't give advice unless asked.

Again, George Washington: "Go not thither, where you know not, whether you shall be welcome or not. Give not advice without being asked & when desired do it briefly."

ONE OF THE HARDEST things for young children to do is to stand firm in their beliefs. –Especially when trying not to offend others or trying to avoid being rude in the course of conversation. A real man models these types of interactions in the presence of his children. Why? So, when they become adults, they have hopefully learned the skill of *bold conviction.*

Bold conviction is not to be confused with rudeness or anger. It's simply standing firm in your beliefs regardless of the opinions of others.

To be bold in your convictions, avoid riding the fence on issues that are considered inflammatory. Calmly and rationally state your belief and don't press the issue to the point of rudeness. For example, politics used to be a conversation piece at family gatherings that could be part of a civil discussion. Now, no one wants to offend anyone so nobody talks about anything of substance. In fact, real men used to discuss matters of family, state, religion, and even philosophy. Now we've degenerated to talking about sports, man-toys, and weather.

I remember, long ago, being a new college student. I'd waited a long time to begin my education and was excited to finally be moving forward towards that goal. Part of being a new student is of course completing the general studies requirements. One of the first courses I took was Philosophy.

For the most part, I enjoyed this course. I was exposed to, and greatly enjoyed (and some not so much), some of the writings and essays from the greatest thinkers in history: Machiavelli, Douglas, Jefferson, Thoreau, Plato, Aristotle, and several more. However, once Jesus was brought up as a "great thinker" in a class debate, the Professor argued that Jesus was not considered a great contributor to critical thought since he drew upon the knowledge of his ancestors; and, according to said Professor, was not particularly contributory to anything original. The professor wasn't condescending or rude; rather, spoke his opinion with a sincerity of fact.

If memory serves correctly, I remember seeing several heads nodding in agreement; though I certainly did not agree. However, since I was not yet a born-again Christian at the time, I did not argue the fact. –Someone else did.

I remember another student timidly raising her hand and stating that she did not agree with the Professor. He politely allowed her to speak then began citing his reasoning as to why he believed the way he believed. I wasn't particularly convinced when he was finished, and the young student who had objected did not pursue the issue any further. I waited for her to argue her case, but she did not.

Everything in me was screaming, "His argument doesn't hold any factual truth, why don't you say so?" However, I did not voice my opinion either, and held my peace.

Looking back, I should have stood with bold conviction and supported that young lady. Though I wasn't declaring my faith at the time, I knew enough about the Bible and the teachings of Christ to know that he most certainly was considered a "great thinker" during his time, and was considered very wise even among his contemporaries. Even the Sanhedrin found themselves at a loss for words when rebuked by him over matters of religious teachings.

As the years have gone by, I've used this lesson to ensure I always remained a man of conviction, and bold in my beliefs.

Real men don't use phrases or expressions that diminish their true beliefs. Such as:

1. "As long as they don't bother me. It's all good."
2. "It's not my place to say."
3. "People can do whatever they want. It's a free country[23]."
4. "What people do is their own business."
5. "I don't want to offend anyone."

The last one is my personal favorite. If you have to constantly be worried about what you say as offensive, then what's the point in even speaking?! Again, I'm not referring to talking in anger or being rude, but simply staying bold in your beliefs. For example, if I am approached and asked a simple political question of whether or not I believe the federal government should confiscate all guns as Australia did, then my answer is firmly: No. I'm a conservative and believe in the constitutional right to bear arms. I would not dodge the question or say "I don't want to offend anyone." Be a real man and state your opinion when it is asked of you.

I have respect for American men who are gun abolitionists. At least they state their beliefs with conviction. But again, I condone no one's actions that cannot express their beliefs with civility.

Be bold in your beliefs. Be a real man. Stop whimpering behind the excuses that make you look small and indecisive. Look me in the eye and speak with conviction. Be true to yourself and not cower to the pressures of others who feel they have the right to suppress your beliefs.

When children see an example of bold conviction, they see a real man in action. Not a man who is violent at the spark of any argument, rather, a man who stands for his beliefs with civility and respect for others. This is the social ingredient sorely missing in the modern era.

Always be a real man of conviction and civility. Teach this to your children. They will be grateful as adults for your investment in them.

MOST ASSUREDLY, AMERICANS could be more civil towards each other; especially to those less fortunate.

There is an expression that goes, "In America, even the poorest man lives like a king." Compared to the squalor people are forced to live in around the world, to literally die of starvation and malnutrition, even homeless people in the U.S. look pretty good. This isn't to demean the homeless plight in our country, but it definitely lends perspective.

Another perspective we need to teach our children is the difference between *want and need*.

**A real man will always clearly define the difference between want and need.**

As adults, we sometimes fool ourselves by turning a luxury into a need. For example, you do not need a home gym or gym membership to stay physically fit; you just need to commit to an alternative workout plan. Yet, it's just as easy to convince yourself that you need to buy a home gym because "it's necessary for me to get into shape."

When we try to explain this to children, it is difficult for them to grasp. In a culture driven by consumerism and the poor quality of material goods to ensure the engine of consumption never stops, all children see is perpetual purchasing of "stuff." The latest and greatest cell phones, tablets, computers, and other media tools.

–The newest model cars, clothes, ATVs, and bigger and better homes.

The sheer volume of material things available for us to purchase, overwhelms our ability to effectively filter what is a need or a want by simply talking to our children. Therefore, we must also show by example even as we pause to explain to them why.

At one point, my youngest son and his sister *really* wanted a "cool and awesome camper" like other people have. Because we enjoy the outdoors and like to go camping, they see people use nice campers while we always use a tent.

"When can we buy a camper, Dad?" Emily asked once on camping trip.

"Yeah!" Ethan chimed in. "That would be awesome!"

"If we ever buy a camper," I answered with a laugh, "it would have to be on the one-payment-plan."

"What's that mean?" Ethan asked.

Always eager to use a teachable moment, I sat my children down beside me and pointed to several of the campers set up within the camp ground.

"Look at all these campers around us. There are small ones, large ones, new ones, and over there, is an old one."

"Of all these campers, which one do you think you'd like to have the most?"

"I like that really big one, there!" Emily pointed.

"I like the color of that one," Ethan also shared.

"Of all the ones here," I explained, "I'd probably take the old one."

"Why would you do that," Emily balked. "All these new ones look better.

"Well, of all these campers, that one is probably paid for. It may not be new, but it looks to be in good condition. It's well taken care of on the outside, so probably it's in good shape on the inside. But like I said, the most important thing is that it's probably paid for."

"Why is that important," Emily pressed.

Instead of answering, I asked another question instead.

"What do you think all these people do with their camper when they go back home?"

"They park it in their garage," Ethan replied.

"Right. And when I say it's not paid for, I mean they borrowed money to purchase the camper, and then make a payment to the bank once a month until all the money is paid back. It's possible," I continued, "that some of the people out here are retired and have paid for their camper, but most are probably making payments. So that means for most of the year, they are paying for something they are not using; and that is not a good financial decision."

It took a moment for the lesson to sink in, but eventually I could see understanding in their eyes.

"In other words," I said, "having a camper is a *want* not a *need*. So, if you are going to buy a camper, be sure that you can pay cash for it all at once."

**Real men never borrow money for a want, and always place needs first.**

When teaching the difference between needs and wants to children, it is difficult to explain the difference. To truly help them comprehend this critical skill in life, you must be a real man and set the example. If you choose to lead a life of debt and excess, then this will be the habit your children will most likely inherit.

NEEDS AND WANTS ARE something we all struggle with, but if we stay on the path of the real man, we will remain a contributor to our families, and not a parasite.

Contributing to the family is critical to the development of children. By doing so, they feel part of the family unit. Contribution usually comes in the form of work. Simple chores at first, and as they get older more laborious tasks can be trusted to them.

With our children, my wife and I set the expectation that they will do certain chores. These chores range in variety from making their beds, to emptying the dish washer. With this, they have the opportunity to get paid an allowance. Each chore earns them a specific percent of their total allowed allowance for the month. They are not paid for the chore. This must be done regardless as a contributing member of the family. They are paid for the work if it is completed in a timely manner. If not, no pay. At first, this concept was not easy for them to grasp; but once they were paid the first time, and did not receive all their allowance, they soon understood that timely work meant full pay. So far, this method has been effective and allows me to teach several lessons:

1. Hard work equals reward.
2. As a member of the family, you are required to contribute.
3. Financial management.

As my children have gotten older, they have progressed to greater responsibilities. However, the expectations are still the same.

**Real men require contribution from their children, but do so fairly, and with love.**

THROUGH HARD WORK, children learn the lesson that everything in life comes with a price. Most times, the price is paid willingly as we work hard to succeed or excel. However, there are other times when the price is very painful because of unwise decisions. For this reason, we need to be life-long learners to overcome our ignorance. This is the most difficult concept to pass to our children. Personally, this was not passed from my parents to me, rather, from a mentor who was willing to stress the importance.

A large part of being a life-long learner is being willing to do research and to seek guidance *before* making big decisions. As simple as that sounds, you'd be surprised how many big decisions are made without any due diligence. –Quitting a job, buying a home, another car, getting married, starting a business, opening a credit card account, getting a pet, buying a boat, etc. All these things have the potential of significantly impacting the family. –Either financially or adding significant stress to the routine of life. For example, if both parents work and the children are in school all day, it may not be wise to have an indoor dog. Or, if your debt-to-income ratio is high, it may not be a good time to get another credit card.

Being a life-long learner implies that you will exercise wisdom and discernment before making decisions you are ignorant about; and passing this skill to children is not just the most important thing for them to learn, but the most difficult for you to teach. **Real men set the example of a life-long learner so that their children acquire the skill.**

A REAL MAN TEACHES his children. Period.

There is no greater cause, purpose, activity, or event that supersedes this responsibility other than salvation. Material wealth, possessions, property, and prestige mean nothing. Power, dominion, empires, and conquest mean nothing. There is no success to a real man's life without the success of his children. Fore when the end comes and the last breath escapes our lips, we should all use it to utter the words, "I have done all that I could for you beloved children. Do the same for yours."

# 11

# Real Men Can Manage Money

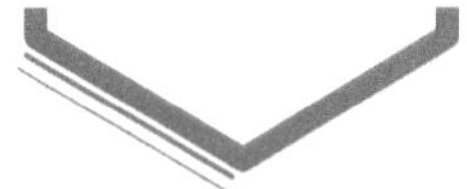

"He who loves money will not be satisfied with money, nor he who loves wealth with his income; this also is vanity."
Ecclesiastes 5:10, ESV

Money is a major cause of failing marriages. If a man does not have the ability to manage his money prior to vowing fidelity, then he is most likely doomed to fail his wife and family.

Let me be utterly clear and pointedly blunt:

**You are not a man if you do not have control of your finances.**

The first lie a man will tell himself is, "I don't make enough money so I always have problems paying the bills." This is an excuse to resign to apathy. –An excuse to bury one's head in the sand and wish problems away.

Men are born natural fighters, and want to effect change. A man needs to tap into this instinct, roll up his sleeves, and fix the problem. It's what we do as natural problem solvers. Men who choose to ignore this instinct are not being men.

At our poorest time, my wife and I never faced utter ruin. Yes, I made some financial blunders, but I learned from them, and didn't repeat them. And to my memory, we only ever asked family for help once our entire marriage.

In 2001, I was working as a teacher in a very small and rural elementary school in North Carolina. Truth be told, it was the best teaching assignment I ever had. The children were very well behaved and eager to learn. Unfortunately, I was laid off once the school year ended. The student population declined, so not all the teachers were needed. –And there were no other positions available in the county. To make matters worse, I was under the impression that my pay was being adjusted to continue over the break[24]. It wasn't. Of course, I should have checked based on my contract, but failed to do so. These events led my wife and I to an emergency family meeting. We knew that things were about to get rough. We had no savings to speak of, very little groceries in the house, and were not going to be able to make the car payment.

We did an analysis of our finances, and the only real problem was my student loan debt (which I deferred), paying our rent and utilities, groceries, and gas money. We figured, if I could get a summer job, we could squeak by until I found another teaching job.

I quickly applied for and got a job waiting tables. Bill time came and we had enough to cover everything but groceries or the car payment (the Jeep Wrangler). We bought groceries. This cycle continued until, just before the school year was due to begin again, the car was repossessed. The lender certainly called asking for the money, but when we declared we were going to choose to eat rather than pay for the car, the lender opted to take it back early.

The point of this story is, we still had another used, and paid for, car. How much better would it have been if I'd been a disciplined steward of our finances and never borrowed money for another vehicle we couldn't really afford? How less stressful would it have been, even though I had to work a summer job, knowing we wouldn't lose our car? –Or about damaging our credit? But, "you were making your car payment fine until you lost your job," some would argue. This is dangerous thinking that I learned the hard way. Making enough money to pay your bills simply means you're living pay check to pay check. And at any moment, you could face financial ruin.

**Being able to pay your bills does not equal financial stability.**

The financial crisis of 2008-2009 caused financial ruin for many. Over 4 million homes were foreclosed on.[25] Jobs lost translated into homes lost. However, mortgages are not a good measurement of your consumer debt since historically homes appreciate in value, but payments still must be met; and if your one month away from missing a mortgage payment, you're broke.

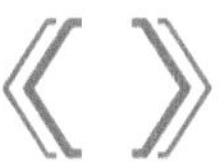

A FEW GENERAL RULES for maintaining financial stability are below, however there is much more to managing and growing money; and a man is obligated to do the research for not only building a financial nest egg, but to eventually get and stay debt free:

| DEBT | YES | NO |
| --- | --- | --- |
| **Mortgage** | Married | Single[26] |
| **1 Car Payment** | Married[27] | Single[28] |
| **1 Credit Card** | Married/Single[29] | |
| **Recreation Vehicles** | | Married/Single[30] |

A mortgage, credit cards, and unnecessary toys are the biggest expenses that typically get undisciplined men in over their heads financially; especially credit cards and the recreation toys.

There are exceptions to every rule. For example, if you are single, and have been for most of your adult life, there is no reason to not enjoy the privilege of home ownership. You may even be able to pay cash if you've wisely saved up enough. But, if you're twenty-five and have only lived in an apartment for a few years and are thinking of taking a mortgage to buy a home, you shouldn't. Save your cash, work hard, and then put fifty to sixty percent down ten years later. Once you do that, double your mortgage payment to pay the home off early.

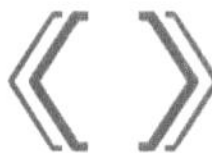

A BUDGET IS A MUST. A budget also includes both incomes if your spouse works. But first, you might be a man if you:

**Set an honest budget and don't lie to yourself.**

A real budget accounts for every single penny that comes into the home. *Every* penny. Paying your bills each month, then blowing the rest is not a budget. That's living paycheck to paycheck. And though it might be fun to blow your money at the clubs or on crap that never holds value long term, the bubble will eventually pop. –A job layoff, a new child to feed, unforeseen medical bills, and the fun is over. If you're not financially stable, you go down with the ship. To get started immediately to affect change, do these two things:

Rule one: Pay yourself first.[31] You *must* have an emergency fund that can bail you out instead of using a credit card.[32]

Rule two: Budget for all expenses. -Fixed costs and variable costs.

Fixed costs are costs that you pay every month. –Electricity, water, car payment (if applicable), rent or mortgage, etc. Variable costs are groceries, clothes, auto expenses, fuel, home repairs, etc. These are all averaged on a twelve-month basis. If you are just starting your budget, then go back into your bill history as far as you can go and average. Once you have done this, then also grant yourself an allowance. Your wife gets an equal allowance if you are married, and it doesn't matter if she works a job or not! Do not spend over your allowance. Use your allowance to save for the luxuries you want. For example, if you want a new tablet, don't just blow money on it, save for it using your allowance.

Finally, commit your budget to paper (or to a computer file as I prefer) and stick to it! Be a man, and don't stray from your financial discipline. Review your budget monthly for the first six months, and then at least bi-annually after that.

But what if I'm married and my spouse doesn't want to play? Then tie her up and throw her out the door! No. Not really. Be a man and explain to her your plan for saving the financial future of your family. If she still resists after that, then it sounds like you need marriage counseling first. Do it.

THERE WILL BE TIMES in your life when not-so-bright people try to lecture you on how to spend or manage your money. There will be other times when relatives or friends try to do the same. Resist.

## A real man will not allow other people to manage his money for him.

One of the saddest stories I ever heard was of a young Army Reserve soldier that I supervised who worked hard while his mother spent his paychecks. This is despicable and unmanly.

In 2001, twenty-year-old Colin was hired as a new Wal-Mart deli employee. His mother, ever the controller, finally relented to allowing him to work; even if it was only for her greed.

Colin was happy. At last he'd be able to earn money.

After the first few months, Colin approached me in regards to his frustration about not seeing very much of the money he was earning.

"I'm working my guts out, and barely have anything to show for it," he complained.

"Are you budgeting your money? Where are you spending it all?" I asked.

"Well," he finally admitted, "Mom takes money for rent and some food and stuff. I get what she says is left."

"How much do you pay for rent?" I asked.

"Well, .... I really don't know. She says she takes enough money to cover all my share, and then gives me the rest."

"Why don't you try asking her what you should pay for rent and food and you give her the money?" I asked. "This way you have more control on managing your budget."

Colin hesitated then finally admitted, "My pay is deposited into her bank account. She manages it for me."

"You don't have your own bank account?" I asked incredulously.

"She said it would be easier for me to help pay the bills if everything was just going to her bank account."

Colin was looking embarrassed. So, I decided to be careful with the rest of our conversation.

"Look, Colin," I finally replied. "You need to make a few changes. I'm sure that your mother is trying to do the right thing, but as a man, you need to be able to manage your own money. You need to open your own checking account and have your money deposited into it."

"She might not be too happy about that," he exclaimed.

"Well, maybe not," I said. "But after all, you're a grown man and it's your money. You should be the first to budget your money and to make the decision as to where you want to spend it."

"If you want to have more control of what you do, maybe it's also time to consider finding your own place to live?" I pressed. "There are several other single soldiers that would like to have a roommate. Why don't you consider sharing an apartment?"

Colin look dejected for a moment, then nodded half-heartedly. I knew at that moment he didn't like my answer or was too afraid to challenge his mother in regards to her using him for financial gain. –And true to my original hunch, years went by and nothing changed for young Colin. In fact, when his enlistment time finally came to an end, predictably he did not re-enlist; and he continues to work the same job living under the same arrangements.

THERE IS GREAT WISDOM in seeking the consultation of trusted friends and maybe some relatives when you need to make a large financial decision. However, a man *must* know that he is ultimately responsible for his own financial wellbeing.

Children who were born in the 1930's were parents in the 1950's. This was my grandparent's generation. Austerity was the preferred method of living because of the lessons learned by their parents during the Great Depression. My mother shared stories with me about how strict it was when raised by her parents. Born in the 1950's, she farmed and worked hard raising her siblings as the oldest. Her father and mother were also factory workers all their lives. Extra money in the house was never an option and spending on the luxury of entertainment was almost taboo. This is the lifestyle she inherited.

To the point, A budget was considered an absolute and an expected skill that, as a man, you should have when raising a family; or setting out on your own to pursue career interests. Each generation wasn't allowed to live on the backs of those who came before them. This is the complete opposite in modern society where men avoid financial responsibility.

Be a man. manage your money. Don't let it manage you. Rise to the occasion. Redeem yourself and your manhood.

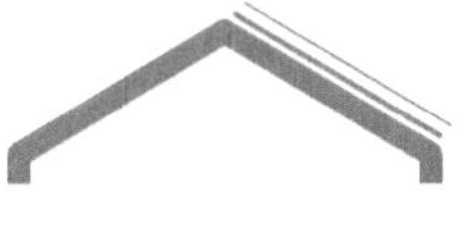

# 12

# Real Men Are Not Whiner's or Liar's

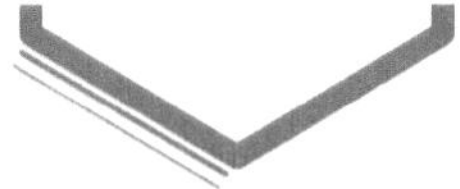

"What is desired in a man is steadfast love, and a poor man is better than a liar."
Proverbs 19:22, ESV

It is unmanly to whine. It is also unmanly to lie. Nothing is as detestable or as irritating to others as a whiner or a liar.

When a man whines, it's usually because something requires work. Financial stability, education, happy marriage, obedient children, promotion at work, a better job or different career, home or vehicle maintenance, attending community or family events, etc. The inner boy takes over and the man disappears.

The definition of whining is to complain in an annoying way. It is the opposite of manliness. It is an affront to what a man should act like.

Real men are not comfortable around whiners. It rubs them raw. It takes an effort not to lash out and rebuke those who are doing the whining. –Because from a real man's point of view, most problems are self-inflicted.

**Real men do not participate in "whine-fests," but are patient with those who do.**

As a man, you need to keep yourself from whining. To do this, you must view every challenge and obstacle with perspective. In other words, is what you are upset about something important, or are you just irritated about something trivial?

Are you broke because the world is against you, or is it a result of poor decisions? Do you whine about your job and blame others, or should you set some new goals and work towards another career? Do you whine about your marriage and kids, or should you work harder at being a better husband or Father?

Are you being a real man and eliminating the whine? There are very few things in life that happen to us that are not the result of decisions we make every second of every day. Driving to work and getting hit by a drunk driver is not your fault. Leaving late for work and getting into an argument with someone that you think is driving to slow, is.

**Real men accept responsibility their decisions and the consequences that follow.**

The greatest whiners in the world, in my opinion are social justice warriors. They believe every problem is the symptom of social oppression. No one wants to be responsible for their own actions, and whine about how to "affect social change." Nonetheless, I will accept that issues relating to children are legitimate and real, because children are rarely able to influence their surroundings; and are at the mercy of their parents' or guardians. Yet, once you become an adult, it is within your personal power to influence you future and to change it. This is a fact. History is full of Americans who have overcome insurmountable odds to improve their lives. They didn't whine over their circumstances.

If social justice warriors *really* want change, they will focus their efforts on the children of this country, and let grown adults be responsible for their own actions. –And thankfully, some charitable organizations do.

American men who whine should be ashamed of themselves. In our country, everybody lives pretty well compared to other countries. There is really no excuse for not leading a wholesome and fulfilling life. Every opportunity is extended to each of us equally. We have constitutional freedoms that grant us liberty of movement, economic pursuit, and speech.[33] We also have the privilege a free public education.[34]

One of the negative sides to being a soldier is seeing the absolute depravity that children are forced to endure around the world. It is a wrenching reminder that, as Americans, what we view as poverty is nowhere near what *real* poverty is.

During the summer of 2010 in Iraq, I was part of a mission that involved conducting a convoy from Baghdad to Balad. We were tasked with inventorying bridging equipment in preparation of taking custody of it all for a Unit that was due to leave the country. As with every convoy during the war, it was always a crapshoot whether or not you would hit any IED's. Thankfully, though, we had no encounters that day.

Along the route, we passed the open dump where all of the trash for Balad was disposed. –And judging from the massive mountain-size piles, it was an area that also serviced Baghdad's trash.

The landfills are left open because the cost of burying the trash was too expensive. So, to overcome the growing piles, they were set on fire and left to burn all the time. The smoke and smell was so thick it choked you. In fact, when coalition forces drove through this area, every effort was made not to breathe the particles in the air.

On the way to Balad, we of course noticed the burning trash, but it was the trip back that made an impact on me.

Stiff from sitting, I tapped my gunner and took his position just to get a view and to break the monotony. From the gunner hatch I could see the mountains of trash more clearly. As we passed them, traffic slowed significantly as our convoy worked around civilian vehicles. While this was happening, I was sweeping our position very closely; as it afforded an opportunity for insurgents to toss RKG's (*Ruchnaya Kumulyativnaya Granata* - handheld shaped charge grenade) down the open gunner hatch. While doing so, I couldn't help observe eight or nine children digging through the trash. These children are part of the homeless in Iraq. –Beggars that live on the street and eat anything they can find in most cases. If they are lucky, they are sent to orphanages that can care for them. Sometimes, though, the orphanages are worse than the streets.

The children looked gaunt and painfully malnourished. Their clothes looked ragged and torn. –Skin stretched thin across all-to-visible bones, and some of them had several open sores on their arms. In their sunken eyes, I could see desperation and fear. I could tell they were considering running after us to beg for food, but our vehicles were crossing a low-level bridge in front of them, so getting nearer to us was impossible.

In the twenty seconds or so we paused in front of them, I could see a lifetime of pain. I could see in their eyes the struggle of survival that no child should have to endure. It was heartbreaking. I didn't even have time to throw an MRE. –Something soldiers often did for the children.

This is something seen in every war. –And as stated before, it gives you perspective. It also changes you and affects you your whole life. It makes whining about anything seem very trivial.

**Real men know the difference between inconvenience and desperation.**

BE A REAL MAN, DON'T whine. Honestly determine your options when examining your circumstances. Don't succumb to the temptation to whine. Because unless you are digging through human refuse to eat, you're not desperate yet. To others who have witnessed real depravity, you look like a fool. You look weak and unmanly.

If you are in a place where you feel you just can't go on, remember that others in this world have it far worse. Seek help through the support of others, and advice from those who are qualified to give it; but do not expect them to provide resolutions to your problems. That is your job. Be a real man and don't be a whiner.

THOUGH MEN WHO ARE whiners are unpalatable, even worse are liars. We all struggle with the smallest of lies. It is the human condition. Nonetheless, I'm referring to liars who have significant and harmful effect on other people. –Liars who cause great harm to friendships, marriages, and the community.

**Real men labor to be as honest as humanly possible.**

One of the most painful experiences you can have in life is dishonesty from a close friend.

There are few people in our lives we open up too. –I mean *truly* open up too. I have four such friends. I have many good friends, but only the aforementioned know almost every detail of my life. These friends I trust explicitly. The trust I have instilled in them has never been violated. Nonetheless, not everyone has been as fortunate.

Judas betrayed Jesus, Brutus betrayed Caesar, and in both, friendships were in place. Yet also in both, disaster occurred when the friendship was violated.

Have you had a Judas in your life?

**Real men never compromise the trust of a friend.**

Friendship is a powerful weapon. It can provide stability to your life and be leverage for community and career happiness. It provides a deeply personal confidant that is not judgmental or interested in emotionally wounding you. Nonetheless, most people are not willing to pursue close relationships except with those they love or are married to.

**A real man will never lie to his wife.**

As a man, to lie to your wife is the worst of sins. This is a no compromise issue. Marriage is an all-in deal. If this is not for you, then don't get married.

The divorce rate in the United States is deplorable. But the cause is always the same: Lies and deceit. It may not be infidelity, but it always involves one partner or the other's dishonesty about something. There can be no secrets in a successful marriage.

WHINER'S AND LIARS are unmanly. Be the architect of your life and get rid of the whine. Be a real man and work daily not to lie. Perfection will never be yours, but the pursuit of it makes it all worthwhile. If you're looking for a starting point, then confess in the Lord Jesus and ask forgiveness for your sins. Once that is done, then chasing your sanctification will yield the results you are looking for. Others will see your example and seek to be around you because of your uniqueness. –Not because you are any better, but rather, because you choose to be different by serving the one true God.

~ End ~

# Epilogue

If you took offense to this book, that was not my intent. Nor was it my intent to somehow model myself as the "real man." Only Jesus can claim that title. Nonetheless, there is a crisis of manhood in America. Whether or not you agree with everything in this book is not important. What is important is the resurrection of men who are willing to lead again.

If a single point was being made, it would be *example*. I call every man to look deep within his soul and light the fires to reclaim our national manhood. Only we can turn the rudder of the sinking ship we now find ourselves on in this country. We are doomed to drown in our own lethargy. We must take a stand for the future of our children and begin to mold them into men who are worthy of inheriting this great country. Only we can shape the future for the better by first being submissive to God, and then by leading our families. Only we can pull ourselves from entertainment and social media addiction. We must, or our children are doomed to follow our example.

American men can change. We can stand arm-in-arm and quit whining; and be men our forefathers can be proud of. We can again stand erect and look each other in the eyes. –Not with malice or threats, but with mutual respect and camaraderie.

As men, we can set the example of adult discourse by being civil and respectful to each other. We can master the art of compromise and lead productive lives. We can resist the need to be wimpy because a toxic culture falsely says we have to be that way. We can refuse!

Men, I call you to rise and resist the indoctrination that pushes for over-sensitivity in men. We don't need, nor have ever needed, safe spaces. We are what we are by design. We were never meant to be soft in voice, weak in posture, and small in mental stature. We are men.

Be a leader for real change. Set the example and be a real man.

[1] U.S. CENSUS BUREAU, Decennial Censuses, 1960 to 1980, and Current Population Survey, Annual Social and Economic Supplements, 1983 to 2023.

[2] Pettinger, Tejvan. "Unemployment during the Great Depression." April 1, 2020. economicshelp.og. Accessed December 2,2023. www.economicshelp.org/blog/162985/economics/unemployment-during-the-great-depression

[3] Historical development of the U.S. social welfare system. www.ssa.gov/history/pdf/histdev.pdf. Accessed December 31st, 2023.

[4] Genesis 1:3, Holy Bible, ESV, 2001.

[5] *The Go-Getter*, Peter B. Kayne, BN Publishing, USA, 2008.

[6] Name changed to protect privacy.

[7] Visits to local schools were viewed much differently at the time during the 1990's. Visit policies are much different today.

[8] This is not to imply that spending time with un-saved friends or family is a bad idea. Reason must be applied. However, good judgement must always be used.

[9] Name changed for privacy.

[10] Hog Boy was the endearing nickname given to me by my Drill Sergeants because I was from West Virginia.

[11] Ephesians 5:18, ESV.

[12] 1 Corinthians 8:10-13, ESV.

[13] sanford.duke.edu/about-us/diversity-inclusion/safe-space. Accessed January 18, 2024.

[14] As individuals, we must always be cautious that our confidence does not evolve into arrogance. To overcome this, entrust a small circle of friends and family to be the wardens of your life. Give them permission to intercede if they believe you may be going down the wrong path. Make your own decisions, but do so with counsel. This is wisdom.

[15] Pat MacDonald (2014) Narcissism in the modern world, Psychodynamic

Practice, 20:2, 144-153, DOI: 10.1080/14753634.2014.894225

[16] Ironically, I would serve as an Army recruiter many years later in my career. Because of my own experiences, I always took the hard to enlist cases. Oftentimes, I was able to be a dream-saver like my recruiter was.

[17] It is important to note that college is not necessarily the key to a successful financial future. In fact, many technical careers pay much more than those that require degrees. The key is understanding what you want to do, then get the education required to do it.

[18] www.cdc.gov/violenceprevention/intimatepartnerviolence/fastfact.html. Accessed January 18, 2024.

[19] In our pursuit of science and technology, which can absolutely be a force of good, we are getting dangerously close to losing control of our own humanity. This is not a new occurrence, and we have faced such rapid advances before. For example, the First World War spurred such significant advances in our science and technology, that roughly eighteen million people were killed in pursuit of the war.

[20] Now with teenagers, my wife and I had to confront to ever-ballooning costs of vehicles. Gone are the days when reliable used cars can be found easily.

We chose to pass on vehicles to our teenagers that were already paid for by us, but with the condition that they take care of the maintenance, tires, etc. This keeps their skin in the game while adapting to an ever-changing world.

[21] One incident involved loaning 8,000.00 to a family member on a credit card (not a wise decision) so that the family member could clean up their credit. The result was not good and ended up hurting my credit when payments stopped. I eventually settled the debt, but never got the money back. However, the relationship to my family is more important, so I never pursued the issue. –Lesson learned? Never lend money to family. Either give them money or don't give. –Never lend.

[22] George Washington, *Rules of Civility & Decent Behavior In Company and Conversation.*

[23] This expression has never had value. Never in the history of the United States has anyone had the right to do *anything* they want to do. If that were the case, then the rule of law would have no merit.

[24] It's a misconception that Teachers get vacation pay over breaks. This is not true. Ten month salaries are divided over a twelve month period.

[25] www.census.gov/history/pdf/2009foreclosures.pdf. Last accessed February 2,2024.

[26] If you are unmarried, older, and well established in a career, then home ownership pursuits are not an issue.

[27] More than one car payment is *never* an option.

[28] With the rise of vehicle cost, this may not always be possible. Don't lie to yourself. Save at least half of the car cost as a down payment if you do take a loan.

[29] For emergencies only. If used, pay off immediately and with one payment.

[30] Exceptions can be made if no longer raising children or retired. However, if you cannot pay cash, then rent one when needed.

[31] Ramsey, David. The Total Money Makeover: A Proven Plan for Financial Fitness, Thomas Nelson Publishers, 2003.

[32] You can never save too much money. Once you have an emergency fund established, continue to save long term as part of your budget.

[33] These freedoms are quickly being curtailed by the forces of socialism that have adversely affected the press, education, government, politicians, and media. Christian men, rise and get involved where you can make a difference.

[34] The current quality of public education can certainly be questioned.

# Don't miss out!

Visit the website below and you can sign up to receive emails whenever Martin Durst publishes a new book. There's no charge and no obligation.

https://books2read.com/r/B-A-ARYCB-SVEUC

Connecting independent readers to independent writers.

# About the Author

Martin Durst lives in West Virginia, and is married with three children. Martin served thirty years in the U.S. Army serving in the infantry, the engineer corps, and as a recruiter. He also worked as a middle school teacher for seven years in North Carolina. He currently works as a construction supervisor for an oil and gas company, and is a certified project manager.